Kaize
Book Two

SHANE EVERSFIELD

Copyright © 2019 Shane Eversfield

All rights reserved.

ISBN: 9781082744273

CONTENTS

	Acknowledgments	vii
	Introduction	Pg 1
1	Mindfulness and Kaizen-durance: A Deeper Look	Pg 6
2	Challenges of Mindfulness Training	Pg 14
3	The Case for RPE: Rate of Perceived Exertion	Pg 25
4	Exploring Neural Fitness Part 1	Pg 35
5	Exploring Neural Fitness Part 2	Pg 44
6	The Endurance Diamond	Pg 58
7	An Introduction to Neural Training	Pg 61
8	Conclusion	Pg 76

ACKNOWLEDGMENTS

Copyright © 2017 by Shane Eversfield. All Rights reserved. No part of this book may be reproduced or transmitted in any form or by any means electronic or mechanical, including photocopying, printing, recording, or by any information storage and retrieval system, without permission in writing from the author, Shane Eversfield. You can email Shane at:

shane@kaizen-durance.com.

Website: https://kaizen-durance.com

Text and concept: Shane Eversfield

Cover Design and Graphic Artwork: Mat Hudson

© Kaizen-durance

First edition published 2017.

Kaizen-durance, Your Aerobic Path to Mastery and the logo depicted on the cover of this book are trademarks registered with the United States Patent and Trademark Office by Kaizen-durance LLC.

Be Here Now

INTRODUCTION:

This is the second book in the series *Kaizen-durance, Your Aerobic Path to Mastery*. In the first book we identified kinetic intelligence (KI) as a most promising resource for the master athlete. KI is the *wisdom* we acquire over the decades that enables us to enjoy continuing growth and mastery, even as we experience aerobic decline.

In this book, we explore the most effective means to accelerate our acquisition of this athletic wisdom. To review briefly, as endurance athletes, we train three physiological systems:

- Muscular
- Metabolic
- Neural

It is our *neural* system that responds and improves the most to training. It is our *neural* system that can continue to improve well beyond our aerobic prime. And it is through our neural system that we develop kinetic intelligence.

Here, in Book Two, we explore neural fitness. As master athletes, by expanding our training focus to include the long-term promise of neural fitness, as we maintain metabolic health, we can:

- Maximize return on our aerobic investment in athletics, and life
- Establish a healthy balance between athletic performance and overall health, minimizing risk of injury, and acute and chronic illness
- Enjoy enhanced athletic performance and life performance by developing a strong union between a healthy functional body and a healthy functional mind

To build this guide, we will explore these questions:

- What is neural fitness?
- How is it relevant to endurance fitness and athletic performance?
- What are the specific aspects of neural fitness?
- How does each aspect benefit endurance training and performance?
- Can we measure neural fitness like we measure aerobic fitness?
- How can we apply our knowledge of neural fitness to endurance training sessions?
- How do neural training sessions differ from metabolic training sessions?

Preparation:

However, before we can begin this exploration, we must build upon the foundation we established in Book 1. We must:

- Look deeper into the nature and function of mindfulness, specifically as it applies to endurance athletics.
- Identify and address the challenges to initiating mindfulness training, and then… staying with it.
- Look again at Rate of Perceived Exertion (RPE) as an optimal way to measure metabolic intensity during neural training.
- Consider ways to develop our skill of accurately quantifying RPE.

Zendurance: Health Multiplied

Combining endurance training with mindfulness training as a single *zendurance* practice enables us to improve and enhance fitness, function and health - physically, mentally and even emotionally and socially. As zendurance athletes, we use the *same* practice session to achieve all of this simultaneously - truly maximizing our return on investment.

In a sense, the childhood activities of swimming, biking and running can now double as our daily *yoga* practice instead of being a daily workout to get to a race finish line. When we transform that daily workout into a daily *mindfulness practice*, we orchestrate the Fitness Cycle more effectively. It serves as more than a way to stress the metabolic system and the endocrine system.

"Wait a minute, did he just say 'yoga' practice?"

No worries! To practice this kind of "yoga", you don't have to wear a white turban and twist your body into a pretzel. "Yoga" simply means yoke or union. We practice yoga to strengthen the union of body and mind. Interfacing your mind and body doesn't require the white turban or the contortions; it happens through *neural training*. As master athletes, we craft PAGES (precise, aligned, graceful, efficient, seamless) strokes and strides through a rigorous *neural interface* of body and mind. *This* is our yoga practice.

Crafting those strokes and strides is an intense and relentless problem-solving activity that constantly challenges and engages our neural system. Medical research has shown that any form of neural exercise can slow the aging process: playing chess, painting, playing a musical instrument, learning a foreign language, swimming. And when that problem-solving neural task involves healthy, sensible aerobic exercise for body and mind together, the benefits multiply.

As zendurance athletes, we improve athletic performance through the mind-body union of *neural fitness*. With this approach, as we strive to improve, we are far less likely to "bang our head against the aerobic wall". That is, we are less inclined to stress our metabolic system too much, too often and for too long, which can be detrimental to our health. Instead, we improve athletic performance by cultivating the *wisdom of kinetic intelligence* and applying it to PAGES. With this approach, we experience kaizen - steadily progressing towards mastery, well beyond aerobic prime.

Experiencing that improvement gives us the motivation to continue approaching endurance training through a seamless interface of mind and body. Measuring progress and attaining goals sparks our *motivation* to fuse mindfulness training with endurance training. We are master *zendurance* athletes.

Neural Training or Metabolic Training

Most of us have invested decades resisting the decline of aerobic fitness, striving to maximize our metabolic potential on race day. If we choose to implement a training regimen that is focused on neural fitness and performance, are we going to lose what we've worked so hard to develop, or at least to preserve?

The purpose of this book is to provide endurance athletes with insight about neural fitness, and to prepare for neural training. However, your training does not have to be an either/or decision. You don't need to give up your long-term investment in aerobic fitness and the precision of your scientifically derived metabolic protocol for the more *intuitive* approach and less metrically exacting procedures of neural training.

You can integrate both types of training in *the same daily sessions*. They can be complimentary and compatible.

If you have a successful and satisfying history with metabolic-focused training - with few injuries, or bouts of training-related illness - you can continue to train as you have. However, you can now enhance that training with a new focus on neural fitness and performance. This will become clearer as you read this book.

In this book, we begin to explore side-by-side the metabolic and the neural objectives for specific types of training. We will continue that exploration in Book 4, "*A Guide to Neural Training*". In that book will also see that it is possible to train neural intensity with *or without* metabolic intensity.

What's Next?

Motivation is a great catalyst for anyone who chooses to engage in *mindfulness* training. And mindfulness training is an *essential component* of neural training. In Chapter 1, we revisit mindfulness and consider how it serves as the foundation of Kaizen-durance. We explore just how vital mindfulness is for athletic performance.

CHAPTER ONE:
Mindfulness and Kaizen-durance: A Deeper Look

Introduction

Let's revisit this thing called mindfulness and look at why it is vital to us as master athletes seeking improvement beyond the years of aerobic prime. Begin with this simple exercise: Pause for a moment… How do you define mindfulness? Write down a very brief description of what mindfulness is for you.

Here is how Jon Kabat-Zinn, the founder of MBSR defines mindfulness: *"Mindfulness means paying attention in a particular way, on purpose, in the moment non-judgmentally."*

I offer one change to this definition. Instead, of *paying* attention, mindfulness means *investing* attention. Investment is a willful form of paying, but it is not to clear a debt, or even to receive an immediate trade. Investments usually yield some return that is more valuable than the investment. Often that return is perpetual, and does not begin to arise until sometime in the future.

At the most stripped-down, bare-bones level, mindfulness is our skill and our strength to BE HERE NOW. That's it. By investing our attention, we fully arrive, occupy, engage and participate in this moment as it is arising.

What can we gain through mindfulness training? We increase our ability to deeply invest our awareness and attention in *this present moment* without distraction - just as the martial arts sensei does when he faces an opponent. We are arriving in this present moment with 100% of our perceptive acuity, ready and able to respond brilliantly. This supports us to maximize return on our investment - in any area of life.

How Do We Train Mindfulness?

We train mindfulness when we practice interfacing our *awareness* with our *attention*.

"Awareness? Attention? What's the difference?" Let's review the subtle but profound difference between these two:

Attention is our perception of what we are focusing on right now. This can be a sense-felt experience, a thought, an emotion, or some combination of these. The undisciplined monkey mind we looked at in Book 1 can shift and re-direct our attention in an instant, like a ping-pong ball ricocheting around. We are unable to direct and hold our focus on one thing for very long.

Awareness is that aspect of our consciousness that exists "outside" of this attention. Being outside of our attention, it is *undetectable* to our attention. That means we can't really sense it. However, when *awareness* is grounded and vigilant, we are able to control and direct the *attention* like a tool. With awareness, we can keep our attention anchored in this moment. Without awareness, our attention bounces around uncontrollably.

The instructions for training mindfulness are simple: When we are aware that the attention has wandered to something other than what is arising here and now, we gently bring our attention back. We gain mindfulness as we:

- Awaken to awareness (again, *outside* of attention)
- Occupy awareness
- Interface awareness with attention and fully invest them in the present moment as it is arising.

In "The Power of Choice" - the final chapter of Book 1 - we recognized that we must make the choice to train and practice mindfulness moment-to-moment, over and over again.

"All this talk about mindfulness. What's it got to do with endurance athletes?"

So Darn *Complex*

Paula Newby-Fraser, Mark Allen, Dave Scott and Natascha Badmann are the living legends - the "samurai warriors" - of Hawaii Ironman. Together, these four athletes were crowned *twenty six times* at the finish line in Kona.

With her final win at age forty (her *eighth* win), Paula was first across the finish line over her younger, more "prime time" competitors largely because of her *kinetic intelligence*, rather than her aerobic fitness. All four of these triathlon warriors, especially Paula, found a way to victory through *wisdom* - through the diligent and patient pursuit of mastery that requires many years of *neural* (as well as aerobic) training.

Let's consider just some of the myriad factors that affect the performance of every endurance athlete, including you. And remember, as your event gets longer, if you disregard any of these factors for very long, the dream of finish line glory can fade very quickly. The variables are many, the consequences are decisive, and the stakes are high!

Here are just some of the factors each of us must be aware of and attend to - both in training and racing:

- Our alliance with gravity using all three of our balance senses: visual, vestibular, proprioception
- PAGES strokes and strides
- Pressure sensing on the surface of our skin: For instance, the movement of water while swimming for the sake of hydrodynamics, the pressure of every foot strike while running for the sake of efficiency and freedom from injury
- Rate of Perceived Exertion (RPE): We will see there are many sensations that comprise this
- Pacing: Even with an accurate GPS, we still must constantly compare and adjust current pace based on RPE
- Hydration, electrolyte and energy status
- Level of discomfort or pain in the many joints, connective tissues and muscles
- Temperature: both internal and surface
- Visual cues about terrain, surface, obstacles
- Auditory cues for awareness of surroundings outside of visual field

We monitor all of these sensations (and many more) as we strive to perform to our potential - often at a stressful metabolic level.

...But, wait a minute. What is this activity we call "*monitoring*"? And how can we improve our ability monitor so many things simultaneously when we are striving to maximize our performance at the high metabolic intensity of racing?

Monitor

As we monitor an (external) event or (internal) sensation, we are *observing* it. It's fairly easy to do - we all have this ability. However, we are tasked with monitoring thousands of minute sensations simultaneously. And, in the case of an iron distance triathlon or an ultra run, we have to be vigilant to all of these observations for many hours.

We may never be aware of it, but throughout our lives, we are actually observing and responding to thousands of events and sensations simultaneously. That's true even in the most mundane circumstances. For sure, not all of these events and sensations require immediate and continuous response. However, to function at a high level, we must simultaneously monitor as many facets of attention as we can and respond judiciously to those that require response. These are skills we develop through mindfulness training.

Monitoring: How-To

Monitoring such a vast array of sensations and events simultaneously is only possible when we interface our observing awareness with multiple facets of our sensing attention:

- Awareness does the monitoring.
- Attention does the focused sensing.

To understand this, imagine yourself sitting in a room watching twenty different video screens at once. Is it possible to be *aware* of so many stimuli at once? It is possible when we train our *awareness* to be calm, still, silent, and continuously vigilant. Mindfulness provides the inner strength so that our awareness can stand vigilant with many different channels of our *attention* simultaneously.

Picture again that wall of TV monitors. These monitors represent all of the facets of acute perception that constitute your sense-felt experience. In the case of triathlon, you are monitoring the vast array of sensations that arise as you engage in one of those "simple" childhood activities: swimming, biking or running.

The great samurai warriors of Hawaii Ironman combined endurance training with *mindfulness training* so that they could monitor and respond to the many facets of their sense-felt experience while swimming, biking and then running at a high rate of metabolic intensity in order to perform at their greatest potential on race day.

How do we as amateur master athletes do this?

So Simple, Yet So *Difficult*

First, we must locate and *awaken* to this awareness within us. We must learn to stand our ground while immersed in the overwhelming activity of our immediate attention. Why is this so extremely challenging? Because *our awareness is not detectable to our attention.*

Awareness is not tangible or measurable.

How can we awaken and engage awareness when we can't see, hear, feel, smell, taste or measure it?

And, to make it even more difficult, each day we are overwhelmed and easily swept away by the immediate challenges and dramas of our lives. Without *awareness,* the unmanaged "monkey mind" just swings from one thing to the next - from one sensation to the next, from one thought or feeling to the next, from the past to the future, from fear to fantasy, from desire to aversion, from judgment to reaction… We're just trying to survive.

Whoa!! With such fragmented frenetic attention, if we arrive in this present moment at all, we arrive scattered, with very little perceptive acuity, and usually for just a brief instant. Without Awareness - with a capital "A" - to stabilize and focus our attention, we are unable to really invest in the present moment, with no chance to experience mastery and brilliance.

Locating or awakening to this Awareness is the most illusive and difficult task of mindfulness training. (Please pause, and then read this sentence again.)

Successfully interfacing Awareness with our darting attention is also really challenging, and requires rigorous training. But as we can see here, this is vital if we want to maximize return on our aerobic investment as athletes, and to maximize return on our living investment as human beings.

How can we awaken to Awareness? How can we strengthen it when it isn't even tangible?

As we considered in Book 1, the ancient traditional practice of sitting meditation is regarded as the most effective way to awaken awareness and train mindfulness. However, it's quite natural for us to feel a strong aversion to the *non-doing* of sitting meditation:

"What!? You want me to sit still and do nothing, with no tangible results? Are you kidding? How can I find time for that when I can barely juggle the activities of each day, and still get in my endurance training?"

"Just sit around and observe my breathing? Not a chance!! I'm an athlete!! There are laps to swim, hills to bike, miles to run. That's enough to add to my life!"

But... What happens if we *don't* awaken to Awareness and strengthen it's ability to control and direct our attention? If we arrive in this present moment at all, it is often for brief fleeting moments, with little awareness and a very scattered attention. Our lives are fragmented and hectic. We connect to the present moment by a very thin thread. And that is why we can't find the time to pause, breathe, and pull ourselves together. That is why we feel overwhelmed and helpless.

It's a vicious circle. What are we to do? Well, there is a...

Solution: Zendurance

It's simple! As master endurance athletes, we can focus on *training neural fitness*. To do this we combine endurance training with mindfulness training. We call this combination "*zendurance training*". In zendurance, by targeting neural fitness, we embed mindfulness training into our endurance training.

Mindfulness + endurance = zendurance.

By targeting neural fitness for athletic performance, we can also:
- Awaken, stabilize and strengthen Awareness
- Improve the perceptive acuity and clarity of our attention

- Increase the number of facets of attention we can monitor and respond to simultaneously
- Maximize return on our investment

Beyond improving our athletic performance and longevity, with the mindfulness skills we develop through zendurance, we can transform the quality of every area of our lives:

- Our relationships and family
- Our occupations
- Our day-to-day activities

Performance Advantages of Embedding

Throughout Book 1, as well as this first part of Book 2, we have considered how combining mindfulness training with endurance training into zendurance training can enhance our performance. To summarize:

- We cultivate kinetic intelligence - wisdom for the master athlete
- We craft PAGES strokes and strides
- With less metabolic and mechanical stress, we reduce risk of injury, illness and burnout
- We improve perceptive acuity in all areas of our lives
- We cultivate and train mindfulness skills that empower us in every area of life
- We maximize return on our aerobic investment… when we *invest* our awareness and attention

What's Next?

In Chapter 2, we look deeper at some of the challenges that can discourage us from training mindfulness, and the empowering opportunities that await us as master athletes when we choose to embed mindfulness training within our endurance training, by focusing on neural fitness.

CHAPTER TWO

Challenges of Mindfulness Training

In this chapter, we explore some of the difficulties that arise as we strive to initiate and then to sustain a practice of mindfulness.

Simplicity

In the introductory book, we considered just how stark and simple mindfulness training is. It is a practice of *non-doing,* a practice of simply *being.* Ultimately, this is how we locate and occupy Awareness: We *pause and stop doing.* In our hyper-busy, hyper-connected information culture, the value of *non-doing* - of pausing to simply *be* Awareness - is difficult for us to even consider as a possibility, let alone appreciate. *"Wait a minute... Remind me again, what's this mindfulness thing?"*

The simple act of just pausing to awaken Awareness and to interface Awareness with attention is so subtle, we just forget to do it - over and over again. Our monkey minds run free while our precious lives scatter like dust in the wind. We are too busy running around trying to collect ourselves - *chasing after our attention.* There appears to be no time or energy to pause and locate that undetectable Awareness in this flurry. This can go on for years, and amount to a lifetime of missing out on fully engaging in this present moment.

It is in the pause of non-doing that we are able to awaken to Awareness. When we do awaken to Awareness, we realize that we are already whole, that there is nothing to collect, nothing missing.

Pressures and Expectations

We live in a culture that measures success by results and goals: The pressure is on! We are expected to provide instant information, immediate answers and quick results: *Action, action, action!!* The demands and pressures of this high-velocity life cause us to *disregard the process of learning and discovery.*

We don't know how to *learn* anymore.

At the root of this? We abhor "not-knowing". We regard those who do not have immediate answers as ignorant, or at least very slow. We fear uncertainty and flock to security. But these cultural norms severely stifle learning and discovery. It takes true courage to be *comfortable with the uncertainty of not knowing.*

It may sound crazy but *not-knowing* is the optimal state of being for learning and discovery. It's a condition of Beginner's Mind.

We need patience and humility if we are genuinely committed to the pursuit of mastery. We need to let go of expectations - both from ourselves and from others - and our obsession with immediate results in order for true learning and discovery to occur.

A detective who is investigating a crime cannot rush to conclusions. Such impatience might result in an innocent person being wrongly convicted. And it may result in a criminal who is free to commit more violations. A master detective assumes nothing. Certainly the goal is to solve the crime expeditiously, but initial assumptions of how the crime might be solved could cloud the detective's perceptions of what is true. Better to start with Beginner's Mind.

A master detective must be comfortable with uncertainty, and patient with *not knowing*. In a state of not-knowing, through the process of investigation, he can exercise the utmost perceptivity and navigate towards the correct solution. The athlete or coach navigating towards brilliant performance through efficient technique must be also be this keen detective, willing to investigate.

The Difficulty of Practicing Mindfulness

Mindfulness practice in and of itself is incredibly illusive and difficult. For proof of that, you need only attempt simple sitting meditation - as outlined in Book 1. Sitting meditation may be the most direct way to train mindfulness, but it is a daunting challenge. How do we awaken to and abide in Awareness, when Awareness is undetectable to our attention?

There is precious little structure or *tangibility* in sitting meditation: *"How the hell do I measure 'Be Here Now'? Where is the tangibility in that?"* In simple, traditional sitting meditation, the tangibility is your *breath* - the sensation of every inhale, every exhale.

Because breathing is something you can do in your sleep, the consequences of breathing without awareness are... inconsequential. No wonder it's so difficult to stay on task in sitting meditation! There doesn't seem to be anything at stake, or any immediate gain.

Again, how can you tell if you are successfully training or practicing mindfulness? How do you know if you are actually improving the interface of your awareness and your attention to optimize perceptive acuity and the functional capacity of your mind?

We live in a "maximize return on investment" culture. If there is no tangible, measurable return in the near future, there is little willingness or motivation to invest. Sure, we may vaguely feel that being mindful in this present moment could gradually yield profound benefits and returns sometime in the future. But as profound as those benefits might be, they are subtle and illusive right here and right now. And they are definitely not recognized or appreciated by our culture.

Isn't there some way to measure it?

Motivation To Train and Practice Mindfulness

Like anything else, to train and practice mindfulness, motivation is essential.

As athletes, we motivate ourselves to train by signing up for events that inspire us (or perhaps *scare* us) to get out the door every morning and diligently turn the wheel of that Fitness Cycle. When the glory of the finish line (or perhaps it's the fear of surviving the ordeal) looms in front of us, we are willing to invest our time and energy to cycle through stress, recovery and adaptation.

As for mindfulness, many people are first drawn to formal traditional mindfulness training as a way to alleviate some form of physical or mental suffering that has not responded to any external remedies. Mindfulness training serves well as a last course of action when all else seems hopeless. This is why Jon Kabat-Zinn initiated the now highly-acclaimed Mindfulness-Based Stress Reduction program (MBSR): He offered mindfulness training to terminally ill patients and chronic pain sufferers through the University of Massachusetts Medical Center.

If we have a clear recognition of the immediate and future benefits of Being Here Now, we are more apt to *practice with purpose* - despite the tedium, discomfort, confusion and boredom that will arise as we train. (The truth is, whether we deliberately practice mindfulness or not, we still experience tedium, discomfort, confusion and boredom in our lives.) As we train mindfulness, we build the calm tenacious awareness to stay with unpleasant experiences as they arise, instead of distracting ourselves or concocting some kind of temporary fix to avoid them.

Besides the alleviation of suffering, enjoyment and satisfaction are also great motivators in our lives. This does not mean you need to be cheery and happy as you train mindfulness - just as you are not always cheery and happy when you are training for your next endurance event. As master athletes, we know that genuine satisfaction and enjoyment are not the same as immediate gratification. A life lived and navigated solely for immediate gratification is not a satisfying purposeful life.

Real, long-term "systemic" enjoyment arises from being *fully engaged*. It also arises as we experience measurable progress and growth: That 20-mile run in the cold rain and sleet may not have been your picture-postcard view of enjoyment. However, back at home you feel the satisfaction of your perseverance, as you move one step closer to the finish line of your goal event.

Few of us are willing to head out into that same wintry mix to run 20 miles without the vision of a glorious marathon finish line in the near future. When there is no "finish line" - no definitive goal to attain - motivation can be hard to muster. However, the finish line of each goal race is only temporary. Then we move on to preparing for the next. It's the same with training mindfulness and pursuing mastery: There is no final absolute finish line, although we may enjoy many temporary finish lines along the way.

Embedding Mindfulness Training and Practice

If we *embed* mindfulness training and practice within activities that have clear parameters, measurable objectives, attainable goals and desirable rewards and finish lines, we are more apt to find motivation and purpose. Taking this one step further, if training mindfulness could clearly *improve the performance* of those activities to help us attain our goals and enjoy the rewards, well… *"Hey!! Where do I sign-up!"*

Most of our life activities - solo or group - are comprised of tasks that engage and challenge our problem-solving skills. Solving a problem masterfully always begins with perceptive acuity - regardless of what the problem is. Clear and accurate perception provides the foundation for effective and appropriate response. *And this is how brilliance arises!* (We all enjoy feeling brilliant, yes? We explore brilliance in the final book of this Kaizen-durance series.)

Any activity can provide an opportunity for kaizen. However, the rewards for engaging in an activity as a pursuit of mastery through mindfulness are highly variable. For instance, mindfully washing the dishes results in… well, clean dishes and healthy digestive systems. And perhaps you get a *"Thank you"* from family members. However, finishing an Ironman results in a glorious finish line scene. There's lots of fanfare, high-fives, tears, hugs, bright lights, a medal draped around your neck, and Mike Reilly proclaiming *"You are an Ironman!"*. (Does this ever happen when you wash the dishes?)

Which one of these scenarios seems more rewarding? The humble domesticity of washing dishes, or the glorious heroics of finishing Ironman? Which one provides a greater service or benefit? And to whom?

Extrinsic and Intrinsic Rewards and Benefits

Recognition and appreciation are great motivators in our lives. There are other rewards and benefits as well. If mindfulness and mastery enable us to engage in our activities - from domestic to heroic - and accomplish all of our goals - great and small - with greater ease and efficiency, that is rewarding even without medals and accolades. After all, we seek to "maximize return on our investment *for a lifetime*".

Rewards and benefits fall on a spectrum between the grand and obvious extrinsic rewards, and the subtle and profound intrinsic benefits. The Ironman finish line is an example of extrinsic reward. As John Collins - one of the 12 finishers of the very first Ironman in 1978 - said, *"You have bragging rights for the rest of your life."* But quietly and patiently training mindfulness doesn't feel like something worth bragging about.

Extrinsic rewards are usually *external*: Tangible and measurable. Perhaps we feel distinguished and admired. Often, these rewards are relatively short-lived. On the other hand, intrinsic rewards are more *internal*: Subtle and underlying, unheralded and quiet. Yet these intrinsic rewards and benefits are often long-lasting, deep, durable, profound.

This is certainly my experience of practicing T'ai Chi. Given the profound intrinsic benefits, my daily practice is simply the best investment I have made in my life. It has endowed me with strength and balance in every way - physically, mentally and emotionally - providing me robust "health *assurance*". I have enjoyed long-lasting intrinsic benefits now for four decades. I am strongly motivated to practice every day. And these intrinsic benefits continue to arise and to expand in ways I never dreamed of. However, these benefits did not arise overnight!

"Kickstarting" Mindfulness Training

When a novice decides to train mindfulness, it is often motivated by *extrinsic* rewards and benefits. As mentioned above, for those beginning Jon Kabat-

Zinn's MBSR program, it's often the desire - or even desperation - to alleviate suffering, chronic stress, or the fear of dying. These are very strong motivators!

However, we don't have to wait for such dire circumstances to arise in our lives to initiate and commit to training mindfulness. For those of us who are not suffering so acutely and with such immediacy, we can embed at least part of our mindfulness training in an activity like finishing a triathlon, or learning to play a musical instrument.

We are initially motivated and inspired by the benefits and rewards of *progress* - rewards that tend to be more extrinsic and measurable. Our reward might be the accolades of a finish line and a finisher's medal, or the ability to play that song we love so much. We are motivated today by tangible results that we may achieve in the near future. Although, there is never a guaranteed certainty.

Even without a guarantee, these immediate, obvious and measurable extrinsic benefits can provide a way of "kickstarting" our mindfulness training: We can embed mindfulness training in an activity that may provide those extrinsic benefits.

Love the Plateau

For the true master - one who is consistent, diligent, patient and committed to mindfulness training and kaizen, the most valued rewards and benefits are usually the most intrinsic - those that are subtle and "systemic". These masters are familiar with the slogan "*Learn to love the plateau.*" When we are on the plateau, we may not feel that we are making measurable progress towards a goal. Decades of mindfulness training and pursuing mastery have resulted in perceptive acuity that enables the veteran to sense and enjoy the most subtle yet profound intrinsic rewards that arise very quietly and very slowly.

Personal Evaluation

Where are *you* in this spectrum of extrinsic-intrinsic motivation?

Here's an exercise:

- Identify those activities, occupations and relationships in your life right now that you value the most.
- List the rewards, benefits, satisfactions you derive from each.

- Look at each of these rewards, benefits, satisfactions and grade them on a scale of 1-10 for how much motivation they provide for you.
- Now look at each of these same rewards, benefits and satisfactions and grade them on a scale of 1-10 for how *intrinsic* (1) or *extrinsic* (10) each one is.

Remember: Extrinsic benefits bring external rewards that are measurable and tangible. Intrinsic benefits bring internal rewards that are deeper and more profound, but subtle and difficult to measure. Extrinsic benefits usually arise faster, but don't last very long. Intrinsic benefits arise gradually, but usually last for a long time.

Now repeat this entire exercise for the activities, occupations, relationships in your life that you struggle with, that you resist.

- Finally, compare the gradings:
- First, make this comparison *within* the list of activities, etc. that you value most. Are the rewards, benefits and satisfactions that motivate you the most extrinsic or intrinsic?
- Now do this *within* the second list - those you resist.
- And finally, compare the two: Which list, if either, has more extrinsic and which has more intrinsic?

Generally, someone new to Practice and Pursuit will appreciate and find motivation in extrinsic rewards and benefits. More immediate gratification. *And that's OK!* Someone who is a long-time veteran will appreciate and find motivation in more intrinsic rewards and benefits. Generally this appreciation arises over years and decades.

The intention here is for each of us to cultivate a suitable and appropriate set of motivations that will result in a consistent commitment to mindfulness training. The secret is *clear vision* of the benefits you can enjoy by training your mindfulness. Discipline arises from clear vision, not from a stern voice or strict rules.

The P.A.G.E.S. Movements

- Precise
- Aligned
- Graceful
- Efficient
- Seamless

Training Mindfulness for PAGES

In Book 1, we explored in depth the many facets of sense-felt experience that guide us to craft PAGES strokes and strides. As master athletes, we recognize the opportunity that arises with each training session for consistent improvement through the patient and skillful crafting of PAGES movements. Given a healthy neural system, there is no apparent limit to how precisely, accurately, gracefully, efficiently and seamlessly we can move our bodies - well beyond aerobic prime.

The greatest resource we bring to our pursuit of PAGES is the successful interface of awareness with attention. We develop this mindfulness through the same *neural* training required to craft those PAGES strokes and strides. We are capable of intense neural activity, rigorous neural training and a high level of neural fitness well into our senior years - indeed, our *master* years.

Proprioception

In Kaizen-durance Book 1, we explored the subtle, yet profound form of *inner* perception - known as proprioception - that serves significantly to orient and guide us in executing PAGES technique. Proprioception enables us to sense our relationship with gravity.

Gravity - like awareness - is intangible. We cannot see, hear, touch, smell or taste gravity.

I have read research stating that *ninety percent* of the neural activity between body and brain serves for proprioception and kinesthesia. (Note: While science differentiates these, I will use the term "proprioception to identify both throughout this book series.) We are monitoring thousands of signals per second just to maintain our alliance with gravity - our balance. As we train, we rely on these thousands of signals per second to engage in the "simple" childhood activities of swimming, biking and running.

If proprioception is so energy intensive and so complex, why is it that we don't seem to pay it much attention?

The truth is we are always *aware* of proprioception. We just don't monitor the proprioceptive facets of our *attention* as closely as other perceptions. Again, imagine that big wall of video screens as the many facets of our attention: We are attracted to other monitors. In our day-to-day lives, we focus a lot more on the monitors that have to do with verbal communication and thought. These are the facets of attention we must rely on to navigate our lives with each other. However, our conversational skills aren't very useful during endurance training and racing.

Gravity and Awareness

Through proprioception, we can *feel* gravity, even though we can't see, hear, touch, taste or smell it. This is how gravity and awareness are strikingly similar:

- They are both virtually undetectable to our five senses.
- Both transcend scale and dimension: They seem to exist from the most microscopic to the most macroscopic and seem to permeate all things.
- Both seem to exist outside of time. That is, they seem to have no beginning or ending.

Here we find a key to the challenge of awakening Awareness (with that capital "A"). Training proprioception is a highly effective way to awaken, strengthen and stabilize Awareness. As master athletes, when we awaken to proprioception as the primary guidance for PAGES, we also awaken to Awareness - the primary guidance for training and controlling attention.

Kinetic Intelligence: Behind the Scenes

There are many, many facets of attention we need to monitor diligently and respond to appropriately if we expect to cross that finish line of the goal race. Crossing that finish line with kinetic intelligence requires two things:

- A calm, strong, stable, well-grounded and vigilant awareness capable of staying on the job for the duration of our event. (Not only are we training endurance and strength for our bodies, but for our awareness too.)
- Enough high-definition monitors (facets of attention) so we can fully interface with the matrix of events that comprise our sense-felt experience - both internal and external.

We cannot cultivate the kinetic intelligence to craft PAGES strokes without Awareness and attention, and without a strong interface between them:

- We awaken and develop that stable vigilant Awareness through mindfulness training, beginning with proprioceptive training.
- We build the wall of high-def video screens and wire them to the Awareness by training neural fitness.

We cultivate kinetic intelligence most effectively by embedding mindfulness training within endurance training. Mindfulness + endurance = zendurance.

Summary

When we combine endurance training with mindfulness training, we can enjoy overall health benefits and sport performance advantages too. These arise together through zendurance:

Endurance training + mindfulness training = zendurance.

We target neural fitness as the most promising resource and viable training method for continuous life improvement as master athletes. The adaptation that occurs through this emphasis on neural fitness results in a stronger and more comprehensive "wiring system" for a more complete body-mind interface. Through long-term neural training, we cultivate and develop kinetic intelligence - wisdom for the aging athlete. As evidenced over the decades at Hawaii Ironman, the top pros out-perform the younger "primetime-aerobic" athletes through this kinetic intelligence.

When we expand our training to include neural fitness as well as metabolic, we can maintain a healthy level of aerobic fitness as we improve PAGES - for decades beyond aerobic prime. Because we are focused more on sharpening neural function instead of metabolic function, we avoid the risky "aerobic razor's edge" that can result in injury, illness, etc.

In our contemporary high-charged lifestyles and results-focused culture, traditional mindfulness training has little appeal. However, with a healthy balance between patient process-focus and sensible goal-setting and pursuit, we can create the motivation that will help us to "kickstart" and sustain mindfulness training. As master athletes, we do this through neurally-oriented body-mind training of zendurance.

Zendurance training and racing provide us with:

- Experience of the functional value of mindfulness training as a way to approach our goals and performance
- Extrinsic benefits that arise from mindfulness

As we experience this functional value and enjoy the extrinsic benefits, we also begin to recognize and appreciate the more subtle, profound and enduring intrinsic benefits that consistent and sustained practice yield.

CHAPTER THREE

The Case for RPE: Rate of Perceived Exertion

The past three decades have produced some remarkable tools for endurance athletes:

- First, it was the advent of the heart rate monitor. By using heart rate as an indicator of aerobic intensity, this tool enables the athlete to train within specific metabolic zones.
- Next came the power meter for cycling. Now the athlete can correlate metabolic intensity with specific power levels while cycling, and compare that to heart rate.
- And most recently, we have GPS units small enough to wrap around our wrists that display pace/speed.

These tools, coupled with ingenious mathematical formulas have enabled coaches and athletes to apply physiological science to train and prepare metabolic fitness for specific events with accuracy and predictable results. They have significantly reduced the element of uncertainty. However…

We've already looked at the sobering truth that metabolic fitness diminishes with age. We have also considered that as we train for the absolute peak of metabolic fitness, we may increase the risk for injury and illness. To train and reach one's highest metabolic potential can be a walk along the razor's edge. This approach requires the athlete to push hard against that advancing aerobic wall.

And there is one more catch with this method: While the tools are reliable and highly accurate at measuring and displaying the metrics of heart rate, power or pace, we must remember one thing: There is a probability that we are not interpreting those metrics as an absolutely exact measure of metabolic intensity. Why?

The Lab Rat

Let's say you go to an exercise physiologist's lab with your heart rate monitor for blood lactate testing to determine your specific lactate threshold heart rate for running. You get on the treadmill, run at progressively higher speeds, pausing so the clinician can measure your blood lactate. At some point your blood lactate level rises quickly. The heart rate at that moment becomes your lactate threshold heart rate. So far, so good!! However…

Your test and the resulting correlation of lactate level to heart rate is for this specific day, at this specific time, at this specific temperature and humidity and elevation, etc. It is lab data, generated while you are a "lab rat". It's specific to the lab. It's also specific to your current "location" in the Fitness Cycle - whether you are still recovering from the stress of a previous training session (or maybe from the stress of an argument with your co-worker, or an upcoming deadline). It's specific to your current energy, hydration and electrolyte levels, how much caffeine you have in your system, where you are in your menstrual cycle…

To summarize: The correlation between heart rate and metabolic intensity that you established in the lab is accurate for that moment. But there is an ever-changing skew between heart rate and blood lactate level caused by lots of variables you cannot control. For instance, if every other variable were held absolutely constant, but the temperature rose by 10 degrees F, that correlation between blood lactate and heart rate may not be the same.

Does anyone train and race in the lab?

RPE: Accuracy in the Field

In my experience, the most accurate way to measure moment-to-moment metabolic intensity is to monitor your Rate of Perceived Exertion, or RPE. This is a fancy way of saying that your most accurate measure of metabolic intensity is based on what it *feels* like to you.

"What!? No hard and fast numbers? You want me to trust RPE over my heart rate monitor and power meter as a more accurate measure?"

This may sound crazy to you. However, some of the the most consistent endurance athletes have relied on RPE as their gauge for metabolic intensity when they train and race. Here are just three well-known triathletes:

- Chrissie Wellington, undefeated in her Ironman career, current course record holder for Hawaii Ironman and world record holder for fastest female iron distance triathlon.

- Natascha Badmann (6X Hawaii Champion) who trains and races completely by feel and gut instinct, and remained a pro into her mid 40's

- Peter Reid, 10X Ironman winner and 3X World Champion at Hawaii

In the early days of triathlon, there were no heart rate monitors, power meters or GPS units to gauge metabolic intensity. Yet the early legends of the sport still claim some of the fastest split times and finish times ever for Hawaii. These pioneers had very little science to rely on, because iron distance triathlon was virgin wilderness. (In fact the entire sport of triathlon at *any* distance was uncharted at that time.) Aside from that marginal science, they navigated the process of training for three different sports (all of them at long distance) *by relying on sense-felt experience.*

The lack of scientific monitors and metrics for those iron pioneers may not have been a limitation. It may have been a blessing. Why?

As we embed mindfulness training within endurance training, our array of sense-felt experiences can provide a very accurate way of measuring metabolic intensity here and now. However, if we are distracted by or dependent upon monitors and metrics, we are;

- less apt to cultivate the necessary awareness

- less apt to develop those specific facets of attention to our sense-felt experience

- less apt to *trust* our own experience

All three of these are essential for:

- Crafting PAGES strokes and strides

- Monitoring metabolic intensity and evaluating that intensity based on current internally perceived capacities and externally perceived environmental factors

- Adjusting pace to respond to that current evaluation, rather than strictly adhering to a mathematically derived plan and a meter or monitor

With practice (and without the distraction that our monitors and meters may cause), each of us can learn to accurately quantify metabolic intensity through an array of sense-felt cues. These sensory cues include:

- Respiration: depth and frequency of breath
- Pulse (Even without a heart-rate monitor, we can sense a slow, moderate, fast or frantic pulse)
- Blood pressure (Yes, we have the ability to feel how much our veins and arteries are constricted or dilated)
- Body temperature
- Degree of ease or stress (both metabolic and mechanical) in specific muscles (Metabolic stress is often felt as a "burn", mechanical stress is felt as strain on joints or tension in muscles)

Developing Your Personal RPE Monitor

You can develop your very own personalized, comprehensive and highly accurate "RPE Monitor" - essential to your zendurance practice   It won't cost you any money, there are no batteries to recharge or replace, and it will not malfunction.

Are you a monitor and metric junkie? Take a courageous leap off the technology cliff by doing some of your training *without* instrument-monitoring your metrics at all. Either leave the instruments home, or cover them up until you *trust* your sense-felt experience and your ability to quantify your effort. (The one exception is for the athlete who tends to consistently overtrain. This athlete can set an alarm on a heart rate monitor to alert when heart rate exceeds a chosen limit.)

The best time to take this leap and adapt to your sense-felt experience is during your off-season activities, and then during your recovery sessions and your base training sessions in the early season.

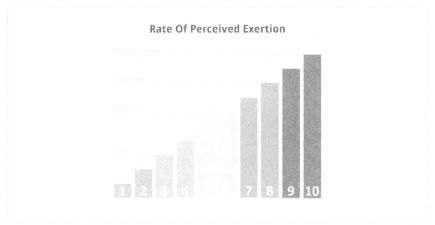

RPE 1-10

To quantify RPE, let's use a scale of RPE 1-10, with 1 being a resting level, and 10 being an all-out effort you can barely sustain for 10 seconds. Each time you train, monitor the facets of your sense-felt experience to determine where you are on that scale at any given moment. (Refer to the list above.)

It's not important that all of us correlate metabolic intensity on the RPE 1-10 scale in exactly the same way. Instead, we each learn to monitor more facets of sense-felt experience more accurately and devise a reliable and consistent means of quantifying exertion that will enable us to adjust our pace and effort so that we can maintain health and achieve our goals.

Below is my *interpretation* of the RPE 1-10 scale. Keep in mind that my race goals are typically ultra distance. Most of my training is at or below lactate threshold - in the range of RPE 4-7. Based on my sense-felt experience, I *feel* lactate building up in my blood (as a "burn" in the active muscles) when I rise above RPE 7. So, I consider RPE 7 to be lactate threshold. I don't train much above RPE 7, except for very short intervals, with generous recovery. Athletes who do train more at RPE 7 or above may be able to sustain those elevated levels of metabolic intensity for longer duration than I can.

- RPE 1- 3: my effort feels very easy with no stress and very little cardiovascular effort.
- RPE 4 - 5: I am in an "endurance comfort zone". The effort is slightly elevated but there is no significant increase in blood lactate and my neuromuscular activity is well-supported by an optimal

cardiovascular environment. My breathing is slow and deep. I maintain RPE 4-5 for multi-day ultras, when I am feeling good. It may drop down to RPE 3 when I feel fatigued.

- RPE 5 - 6: I can feel low levels of neuromuscular discomfort, but it diminishes quickly when I back off just a bit. My respiration quickens a little, but it is still fairly calm. In this range, blood lactate is slightly elevated, but remains steady and does not increase higher, unless I push harder.

- RPE 6 - 7: My metabolic effort is sustainable for 1-2 hours without feeling desperate. My respiration has increased but is not a struggle. (Right at RPE 7, I feel that my blood lactate level is elevated, but I am able to keep it from rising any further. This is the highest effort I can sustain without the lactate elevating continuously. My neuromuscular system can continue to operate in this less than ideal environment for an hour or more.)

- RPE 7+: Above 7, I may hang on for an hour or even longer during a shorter race, but I will feel the accumulation of fatigue. It is building, and eventually I am going to slow down. The longer I push at this pace, the longer it will take me to recover. My respiration is now challenging. (Above RPE 7, my blood lactate level will continue to rise. My neuromuscular is now operating in a progressively less suitable environment.)

- RPE 8: I struggle for enough oxygen, and the burn in my muscles increases noticeably. The pace is not sustainable, and I am operating in an anaerobic state. At and above RPE 8, my blood lactate continues to rise very quickly.

- RPE 9: I can sustain the pace for 30 seconds to 2 or 3 minutes. (At and above RPE 9 the environment can no longer support neuromuscular activity without elevated stress and damage.)

Five-Zone Metabolic Rating system

How does the RPE 1-10 relate to the popular 5-zone Metabolic System? Here is *my interpretation* of it:

- RPE 1-3: Zone 1
- RPE 3-5: Zone 2
- RPE 5-7: Zone 3
- RPE 7: Zone 4

- RPE 8: Zone 5a
- RPE 9: Zone 5b
- RPE 10: Zone 5c

As an ultra endurance athlete, my body is very efficient at burning fat. This means that my *aerobic* threshold (AT) is very close to my *lactate* threshold (LT). For those who are not so fat adapted, there is a larger gap between AT and LT - typically designated at Zone 3. In this zone, blood lactate is elevating, but it is being "cleared" as it is produced. LT is the threshold between sustainable lactate clearance, and unsustainable lactate build. AT occurs near the top of Zone 2. LT occurs in Zone 4.

Make it Your Own

The first step to developing accurate RPE skills is to train your ability to monitor enough facets of your sense-felt experience to feel and to scale your RPE. I suggest that you do this by covering up your monitors and training *by feel*. Again, the best time to make this transition is during your off-season, and during your recovery sessions and base training sessions in the early part of your season.

Once you feel that you are aware of enough facets of your sense-felt experience to scale your RPE, you can correlate RPE to your heart rate zones, power zones or pace. To do this, as you are training, scale your RPE, and then compare that RPE with your instrument. Do this frequently, and at all levels of intensity so that you feel confident relying on RPE.

You may notice that the correlation varies - especially with your power output on the bike, or your pace. Again, the fluctuations result from the many variables that affect your performance - both environmental and internal.

Beware that you may allow monitor metrics to override your RPE:

- If you check your power or your pace and it is lower than you thought it would be, do you feel the urge to push harder, even if your RPE indicates that you are already in the metabolic zone you have chosen to train in? Will you allow your "numbers mind" to disregard your sense-felt experience and take over?

- Or the opposite: Your RPE is lower at a specific power or pace than you anticipated. Do you feel a sense of pride? Or perhaps fear that your RPE is not accurate?

Let go of the need to attain or stick to the instrument numbers and trust your RPE. The exceptions to this advice:

- You are new to RPE
- You have a tendency to train too hard
- You have just finished a goal race

In these circumstances, *be conservative*. Use your heart rate monitor to *limit* your effort, and focus on your sense-felt experience.

I have used RPE as my means of quantifying metabolic intensity for well over a decade - whether I am training for shorter races that emphasize speed (for me RPE 7-8) or for very long ultras that require specific sustainable pacing (RPE 3-6).

Pain and Discomfort

Through zendurance training, we awaken and strengthen a calm, stable, grounded awareness. From that awareness, we are more skillful at monitoring all the facets of our sense-felt experience. We are also able to simply *be present* with discomfort and unpleasant experiences: We are able to experience these sense-felt experiences without resisting, ignoring, judging or complicating them in any way. This enables us to more accurately scale RPE and to respond brilliantly rather than react impulsively - a valuable skill during endurance training and racing. And a vital skill in daily life.

Neural fitness empowers us to be present with all facets of sense-felt experience, including discomfort and pain.

In the endurance world, athletes are seen has having a high pain threshold, or a resistance to pain. These expressions are not accurate. We are simply more able to be present with the experience - the *feeling* - without the compulsion to resist it or change it. (We will explore how neural fitness and neural training empower us to do this later on.)

If we resist or try to avoid discomfort as we train and race, we are more prone to injury. That resistance typically arises in the physical body as tension. Tension diminishes neural function, compromising proprioception and therefore our PAGES. In the mind, our resistance arises as judgment, or an attempt to avoid and block out sense-felt experience. Like tension in the body, this mental break in the body-mind connection also impedes the neural function essential to PAGES.

Summary

Rate of Perceived Exertion is our most accurate and immediate means of monitoring metabolic intensity. There are some inherent problems with relying on external monitors to provide us with metrics for metabolic intensity:

- The testing protocol may or may not be accurate at interpreting the correlation between measured events (such as blood lactate and heart rate or power output).

- The correlations that are established during a test are accurate for the unique combination of a vast array of factors for that specific moment in that specific environment. These will most certainly vary at another time and location.

- The correlations will skew as a result of variations in that vast array of factors. (Example: Heart rate for a specific blood lactate level will be higher or lower than it was during the lab testing.)

On the other hand, our RPE - comprised of many sense-felt experiences - indicates our true metabolic intensity in the moment. We can learn to:

- Monitor an array of sense-felt "data" and incorporate that data into an overall RPE experience in each moment

- Quantify that RPE experience on a scale of our choosing (suggested 1-10)

- Gauge the level of RPE that is appropriate in each moment in response to all internal and external factors and the duration of the event

In the arena of endurance sports, the science of neural fitness is far less definitive and applicable than the science of metabolic fitness. This includes identifying and defining neural fitness, and methods for quantifying and evaluating neural fitness - especially beyond the lab. This lack of science encourages us to rely on sense-felt experience. As pioneers, we get to develop and to trust our own kinetic intelligence and to enjoy the "wisdom" of the aging athlete.

After all, science has yet to identify and measure wisdom either.

What's Next?

In Chapter 4, we begin to explore neural fitness and how it enables us to experience and enjoy *kaizen* as master athletes.

CHAPTER FOUR:
Exploring Neural Fitness Part 1

Introduction

Before we focus on how to train and develop neural fitness, we need explore a few central questions:

- What is neural fitness?
- How does it play into endurance fitness and performance?

In this chapter, we cover:

- A basic look at the neural system and how it functions
- How our neural system *facilitates intelligence*
- The requisite foundations of neural fitness: neural function and plasticity/adaptability
- Engrams: "packets" of kinetic intelligence
- The Engram Process

Let's start with…

Neural Fitness Science: Still a Big Mystery

Science has succeeded very well in defining, identifying and measuring metabolic intensity. This has led to some highly effective protocols for training metabolic fitness to prepare athletes for specific events. Yet, here in the 21st century, science has not yet devised any such methods or monitors for measuring *neural* fitness. (I'm not even aware that science has defined or identified what neural fitness is.)

Without identifying and defining neural fitness, and without the means to measure it in the field - let alone in the lab - the emphasis in exercise physiology will continue to be on metabolic fitness. Yet, scientific research indicates that our metabolic fitness begins to decline at a rate of 1% per year *after the age of 25*. Not much hope for the master athlete.

Some may see this inability to scientifically identify, measure and monitor neural fitness as a deterrent for endurance athletes to optimal neural training and race performance. I see it as a blessing.

Enter the Matrix

All of our sense-felt perceptions and our responding actions are transacted between body and brain through the neural system. This isn't just for athletics, *this is true for every moment of our thinking, feeling and sensing lives.* We don't really need gauges and gadgets to tell us what we are sensing, feeling or thinking. The neural system does this perfectly.

With mindfulness training, we can optimize the functionality and performance potential of our neural systems. We can rigorously train and develop our neural systems without any of the health risks associated with rigorous metabolic training. We can achieve high levels of neural fitness. And we can do all of this without any high-tech tools. How? We accurately monitor and measure our neural function and performance *by using the neural system*. It's *all feeling!*

Again, external monitors and metrics will not aide us here. If we had external monitors for every single one of those facets of attention we considered earlier, we would be so busy scanning all those screens of data, we wouldn't see where we were going! (Like the people we see everyday walking and staring at their cell phone screens.) Our neural system already monitors itself *brilliantly*.

The bottom line: We don't need any advances in science to train our neural system effectively. We simply need to interface awareness with attention, and to fully occupy this present moment. That's it.

Bandwidth

There is however one thing we *do* need in order to rigorously train for neural fitness and to cultivate kinetic intelligence. Actually, it's something we need to *let go* of: Our attachment to how things should be - to our desires and aversions, to our positive and negative judgments, etc.

As we considered earlier, there are many, many vital things to monitor through our sense-felt experience as we train and race. If we expend energy generating a relentless commentary about what is arising, we can't possibly monitor all those facets of attention adequately. The relentless commentary takes up too much *bandwidth* in the neural network. The signal strength and quality of each facet is blurred by this superfluous commentary. The quieter our minds, the more bandwidth we have in the neural network to tune-in to our sense-felt experience. The more we can occupy that incredible matrix of the neural system. This requires mindfulness skills - the subject of Book 3.

For now, let's look at this incredible neural matrix.

Wired

In simple layman's terms, your neural system is a vast network of wires that transmit electric currents or pulses in two directions. The "incoming" currents transmit perceptions - sense-felt experiences. The "outgoing" currents transmit responses. In the simplest model, these currents travel back and forth between body and brain. The "body" end of this network is called the Peripheral Nervous System (PNS). The "brain" end of this network is called the Central Nervous System (CNS).

It's is important to recognize that the CNS includes the spine as well as the brain. This means that your spine can receive and respond to many of the signals sent from your PNS - for instance, from your arms and legs - without relying on your brain to mange the process of perception or response. This includes much of the neural activity that generates your PAGES strokes and strides.

As an example of this: In neuroscience research, a cat with a spinal lesion - a clinical way of saying the researchers paralyze the cat - can still walk on a treadmill if its weight is supported in a sling. How is this possible?

Intelligence: Brain *and Body*

What we call *"intelligence"* seems to be located in our *neurons*. A neuron (as defined on the Wikipedia site) "is an electrically excitable cell that processes and transmits information through electrical and chemical signals." Each one is like a mini intelligence center. Neurons connect to each other to form neural networks. Our brains are densely composed of such neural networks, so it's quite natural for us to experience our brains as the source of intelligence.

However, many of our neurons and these neural networks are located in the spinal cord, and also in the *ganglia* of the peripheral nervous system (PNS). Again, in my crude layman's terms, we can view these ganglia in our arms, legs, hands and feet as "mini brains" that remotely host much of our kinetic intelligence.

Even more intriguing than the paralyzed cat that still walks? The *octopus*, with its *eight arms*. Each arm - and *each suction cup on each arm* - can operate independently from any other. This is possible because *sixty-five percent* of the octopus's neurons are in its eight arms. *The octopus has almost twice as many neurons in its arms than it has in its brain!* Each of these arms can "think" - perceive, problem-solve and articulate - without necessarily consulting the brain. Neurally networking each of these intelligent appendages with all of the others, octopuses are well-known for their ability to escape from aquariums, and to disassemble filter systems - including unscrewing parts from one another.

Returning to humans, here's one more example of our *body* intelligence: All of the neurotransmitter chemicals that are present in your human brain are also present in your gut. Yet, twenty times more neural signals are sent from your gut to your brain than vise versa. No wonder the word for "intelligence" in Hawaiian is *"naau'ao"* - which translates to *"daylight of the intestines"*.

Intelligence includes gut instinct.

So What?

In our context of endurance training and racing, all of this indicates that the awareness and intelligence to move our bodies is - at least in part - located in the spine and even in the ganglia in our arms and legs, and not exclusively in the "penthouse suite" of our brains. Recognizing this changes our experience of what awareness and intelligence are and where they reside within us. It informs us about how we develop and refine PAGES strokes and strides, awakening us to intelligence beyond our normally inhabited consciousness.

At least in part, our motor skills and our kinetic intelligence are located - stored - in our spines and our periphery, rather than solely in our brains. I suggest that awareness and intelligence inhabit not just our brains, but our entire neural network: We think with our bodies as well as our brains. If we recognize this, then we realize that fitness is not just about endurance, strength and speed. Unique to *neural* fitness, it also includes awareness and intelligence.

Neural Fitness

function	plasticity
receives signals	learn to perceive
sends responses	learn to execute

Defining Neural Fitness

Neural fitness *begins* with:

- Neural function
- Neural plasticity/adaptability

Neural Function

The foundation of neural fitness is your ability to generate and transmit electrical signals through your body's neural wiring system. This wiring system must generate clear and accurate electrical signals, and transmit them to the correct destination. As athletes, we rely on this electrical system so that we can execute complex tasks - like swimming, biking and running. (Ah yes, those "simple" activities of our childhood.)

To swim, bike, run, walk, etc., the neural system is transmitting those electrical signals in two directions simultaneously:

- Perceptive signals (including the complex array of neural signals that comprise proprioception) inform the local ganglia and the Central Nervous System (CNS), about what we are sensing from the environment and what is occurring within the body (including how we are aligning with gravity). These signals travel "inward" from the ends of the "twigs" (receptors at the ends of the nerves) to the "branches" (ganglia) or the perhaps to the "trunk" (CNS - spine, brain).

- Executive signals travel in the opposite direction, directing specific muscle fibers and connective tissue fibers to generate PAGES strokes and strides. These signals travel "outward" from the trunk or branches to the twigs.

Our ability to generate and direct these clear and accurate electrical signals (in both directions) is our neural *function*. Given that our neural system provides the interface between perception and action, neural function includes not just mechanical (executive) function but *also perceptive and response functions*. Therefore, as endurance athletes, training neural fitness includes perceptive ability as well as kinetic agility.

Neural Plasticity/Adaptability

Another foundational element of neural fitness is our ability to *learn*. Specifically for endurance athletes, this is our ability to develop and improve our PAGES strokes and strides. It's our capacity for kinetic intelligence. Like neural function, neural plasticity is both perceptive and executive. We must increase our perceptive acuity before we can develop, refine and execute PAGES.

If our perceptive acuity is insufficient, there is no possibility for kaizen - specifically for improved PAGES in our endurance practice. We will continue to execute the same movement patterns we have in the past. *This is why training mindfulness is always a part of neural fitness training:* We must fully occupy and engage in this present moment to maximize our perceptive acuity.

Beyond the athletic arena, as human beings the same is true if we wish to maximize return on our "living every day" investment. As we develop the mindfulness for kaizen-durance, we can apply that mindfulness fitness to every moment of our lives.

Engrams

Pay attention here, because this is where we discover how the neural system develops and "hosts" kinetic intelligence. It occurs through a phenomenon known as *"engrams"*.

An *engram* is "A presumed encoding in neural tissue that provides a physical basis for the persistence of memory; a memory trace." (Quoted from the website **dictionary.com**) The myriad components of your swim stroke and your run stride are stored as engrams in your neurons - specifically in the neurons of your spine and the neurons embedded in your muscles.

These engrams are what some of us experience as "muscle memories" - except that they are really *neural* memories. Engrams are the storage files for our PAGES strokes and strides. They are "packets" of kinetic intelligence. Again, these memory files are stored in neurons - often the ganglia (groups of neurons) *embedded* in the muscle tissue, hence our experience of "muscle memory".

Your efficient running stride is stored not as a single engram, but as an array of engrams. This array of engrams is not stored in a single location, but in a *matrix* of locations throughout your incredible neural network.

Note that the above quoted definition begins "A *presumed* encoding". This implies that engrams are not conclusively proven from a purely scientific perspective (just as science still struggles to define and measure neural fitness).

The Engram Process

Essentially, neural plasticity is our ability to create and manage engrams. Neural plasticity enables us to:

- create
- store
- retrieve
- activate
- coordinate/synchronize
- adapt
- and refine engrams.

Engrams are patterns or programs of behavior/skill/intelligence. As endurance athletes, engrams are the "stuff" of our PAGES from our first stroke through our lifelong practice:

- As we learn something for the first time, we are **creating** and **storing** engrams.
- Then we begin the lifelong journey of practice. Each time we practice, we are **retrieving** and **activating** engrams from a matrix of storage locations to execute each stroke.
- As we retrieve and activate these engrams from a matrix of locations, we must **coordinate** and **synchronize** all of them so that our arms and legs can perform in harmony.
- With each and every stroke we take, we **adapt** the "engram templates" *to the conditions of the present moment.* (The conditions we are adapting to include those within the body, and those of the surrounding environment.)
- The *kaizen* of PAGES technique is our lifelong ability to **refine** the engrams with each repetition of this process during our practice: Each time we run another stride, we learn something from that stride to improve the engrams of our PAGES technique.

Remember, each stride cycle of PAGES technique is processed as a *matrix* of engrams - that is, multiple memory packets. These memory packets are stored in many different neurons located in many places in the muscles/spine/brain. After all, one running stride engages hundreds of different muscles throughout your body.

To summarize, neural fitness includes the plasticity to create, store, retrieve, activate, coordinate/synchronize, adapt and refine engrams. Whew!! That requires a lot of *bandwidth* in your neural network. Each stroke or stride is the result of *intelligence* - specifically kinetic intelligence.

As unique individuals, we may each be very neurally plastic in some areas of skill acquisition and a total couch potato in other areas: Personally, I feel skillful in the engram process as an ultra endurance athlete and as a kinesiologist, but I have very little skill as a marketer. (That is, I have very little experience or skill at creating and processing engrams that enable me to monetize on my insights and experiences.)

Neural plasticity in any specific area is contingent upon training and practice. (Yup, I need more marketing training and practice.) We must engage and challenge the specific neurons that are associated with a skill if we expect to improve. The adage *"Use it or lose it"* applies very well here: Neurons that are not activated and that are not connecting and interacting with other neurons tend to go dormant or die off. If we don't engage our neurons in the Fitness Cycle (Stress, Recovery, Adaptation), we can't expect to gain neural fitness.

CHAPTER FIVE:
Exploring Neural Fitness Part 2

Introduction

In this chapter, we continue our investigation of neural fitness - specifically as it applies to endurance training and racing. Here, we identify and explore:

- Two "dimensions" of neural fitness
- Four elements of neural fitness
- Neural fitness as the essence of kinetic intelligence
- The Four-Stages Learning Cycle

Two "Dimensions" of Neural Fitness

For lack of a better term, I use the term "dimensions" in quotes to identify two distinct aspects of neural fitness:

- Neural function
- Neuro*muscular* function

Neural function refers to the multi-faceted performance of the neural system specifically:

- Perception - both internal (within the body) and external (the surrounding environment)
- Facilitating the Engram Process

The second dimension of neural function includes interfacing with the muscles to express or execute the engrams as movements. We will refer to this interface of the neural and muscular systems as *neuromuscular function*. As we explore the elements of neural fitness, in some cases, we will treat neuromuscular function separate from overall neural function.

Four Elements of Neural Fitness

neural endurance	neural strength
neural speed	kinetic intelligence

Four Elements of Neural Fitness

There are four elements we can train during our daily sessions for neural fitness:

1. Neural endurance
2. Neural strength
3. Neural speed
4. Kinetic intelligence (KI)

The first three - endurance, strength and speed - are familiar to anyone who has focused on conventional metabolic and muscular fitness: Endurance, strength and speed are the venerated components of every endurance athlete's training.

The fourth one - kinetic intelligence, or "KI" - is unique to neural fitness. Our exploration of engrams and neural plasticity in the previous chapter provide some insight into this unique element of neural fitness. KI is an exceptional form of *adaptation* - the third phase of the Fitness Cycle - that we develop exclusively through neural training.

We will return to KI, engrams, and how to train these as part of neural fitness after we look at the first three elements. We begin our exploration with…

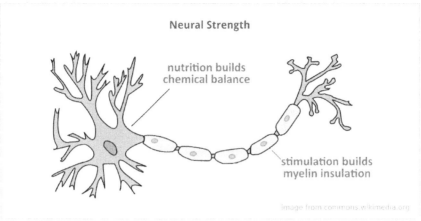

Neural Strength

In the discussion on neural function above, we touched upon a primary aspect of neural strength: The wiring system of our bodies must be strong enough to generate and conduct electrical currents from one location to another. Like the wires in the electrical system of your car or home, the "wires" of your neural system must conduct and insulate:

- The conductive substance (copper is the typical conducting material in your car or house wires) must transport electrical pulses

- The insulative shield that surrounds the wire (plastic is the typical insulating material in your car or house wires) must prevent those electrical pulses from leaking out of the conductive path

Just like metabolic and muscular fitness, neural fitness too requires consistent and appropriate cycling through the Fitness Cycle, and adequate nutrition. When we exercise our nerves (repeatedly sending electrical currents through them) and maintain the correct chemical balance (nutrition - especially electrolytic minerals), we keep them strong and functional. Through the Fitness Cycle, they adapt to conduct stronger currents and more accurate signals.

Insulation is also essential to neural function: Without adequate insulation, the electrical current leaks out of the wire. It becomes weaker and may not ever reach its destination. The insulation on our nerve-wires is called the *myelin sheath*. This insulative myelin aids in the rapid and accurate transmission of electrical currents that carry data from one nerve cell to the next. Autoimmune diseases such as M.S. and A.L.S. destroy myelin sheath and severely impair or prevent nerve function altogether. Myelin sheath is essential to neural strength (as well as neural endurance and speed).

In my personal experience, the most effective form of exercise to build and maintain both the conductive strength and insulative strength of the neural system is T'ai Chi. While this slow-movement meditation may not appear to offer appreciable benefits to endurance athletes, it is an indispensable part of my daily training.

As athletes, if we lack neural strength, it is not just our ability to move our arms and legs to swim, bike and run that is compromised. Our nerves provide interface in *both* directions. When our nerve function weakens, so does our perceptive capacity (including proprioception). And without adequate neural strength, we are unable to process the engrams necessary to generate those PAGES strokes and strides).

Beyond athletics, conductive and insulative strength, are essential for every function in our lives.

"Many Hands Make Light Work"

Many athletes don't realize that when they are performing strength training exercises for muscular strength - such as weight lifting - they are also training *neural* strength. How is this?

When we conduct any form of resistance strength training, we are tasking a specific group of muscles to produce more force. We task that specific muscle group by first activating it via the electrical signals of the neural system. As endurance athletes, resistance strength training is most effective when we train our neural system to *recruit more muscles fibers* to produce the force we need for our sport-specific movements.

Without targeted strength training, we constantly activate *only the same few muscle fibers over and over again.* The active ones must work very hard, while all the others that could be involved remain at rest. When we train the neural system to activate more of the available muscle fibers, we spread the demand out. This means we can generate more force and reduce the risk of injuring the active fibers.

As an example: Amish farmers are known for being able to build a barn in just ten hours *without any power tools*. (You can find time-lapse videos of "Barn Raising" on You Tube.) How do they do it? The *entire community* turns out to build the barn, instead of just one family.

Like the Amish, as athletes, we can recruit more "help" to get us from the start to the finish: We can train our neural system to recruit more muscle fibers to execute the strokes and strides, instead of relying on just a few fibers that do the work over and over again for hours. "Many hands make light work."

Without strength training, many of the available muscles fibers will stay home and lay on the couch instead of getting out there to join the Barn Raising. As endurance athletes, our primary objective in strength training is *not* to increase muscle mass. It is to increase muscle *function*. We achieve this by developing a stronger and smarter neural network. This network results in a stronger more cohesive community - and therefore a much bigger roster of available, capable and willing muscle fibers... and a lot less couch potato muscle fibers.

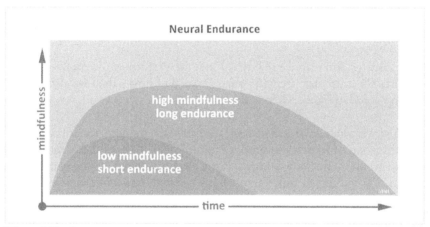

Neural Endurance

Neural endurance builds on the foundation of neural function and strength: First we need great conductive and insulative strength so that our neural wiring system is capable of conducting strong, clear electrical currents/pulses from one location to another. Endowed with conductive and insulative strength, we can develop neural endurance.

Like metabolic endurance, neural endurance is our ability to sustain a specific level of activity for a chosen duration. The most obvious form of neural endurance is our ability to conduct the strong, clear electrical signals over and over again for hours that "express" our PAGES strokes and strides through our muscles. Muscular endurance without neural endurance will not suffice.

However, there are some additional capacities that are unique to neural endurance.

Beyond the biological capacity to generate and conduct electrical signals repeatedly for a long duration, we need neural endurance to manage the Engram Process. The neural system must *retrieve, activate, adapt, coordinate and synchronize specific engrams* over and over. These engrams are the essential KI for each PAGES movement.

As we considered earlier, engrams may be stored in the ganglia of the muscles, the spine and the brain. Regardless of where they are stored, the "data" of each engram must be retrieved and transmitted to the specific matrix of muscle fibers that will generate that part of the stroke or stride. Repeating this task over and over requires neural endurance.

Next, neural endurance also includes the ability to maintain perceptive and executive acuity for a long duration. With neural endurance we maintain high-resolution perceptions and accurate, intelligent responses so we can adapt each PAGES stroke/stride engram to the specific conditions of the present moment - both internal and external. *Much of this occurs through our proprioception.* Therefore, neural endurance includes proprioceptive endurance.

This dimension of neural endurance requires more than just biological function. It is also highly contingent upon our ability to sustain a high level of interface between a stable, vigilant awareness and a high-resolution, multi-faceted attention. In other words, it is highly contingent upon training *mindfulness* endurance. You may begin your most challenging goal event with a strong and functional wiring system, but if your awareness is weak and your attention is scattered, you will lack a vital component of neural endurance.

Finally, we return to the image of the Amish barn raising. When we maximize muscle fiber recruitment for each stroke or stride, our muscular and metabolic endurance improve. Why? We are spreading the work out to more fibers, resulting in less fatigue to each working cell over time.

Neural Speed

Conventionally, speed training is about going faster - with a focus on metabolic adaptation. From a neural perspective, I cannot find any research indicating that we can increase the speed of electrical impulses traveling in our bodies through targeted training. Notably, the fastest neural transmission speeds are for *proprioception and touch* - speeds of 330-350 meters per second (over 250 miles per hour.)

Healthy neural function certainly optimizes our potential for fast transmission speeds. Remember that our nerves require adequate insulation - myelin sheath - for the electrical currents to travel quickly. They also require optimal electrolytic balance.

Neural speed is essential for fast movements, like a fast pedal stroke, or fast leg turnover in a running stride. To realize that faster movement *and also maintain PAGES*, we must be able to retrieve, activate, coordinate, synchronize and adapt the correct baseline engrams at a speed that compliments our mechanical speed. For sure, this is contingent upon how fast the electrical currents can travel through our "wires". Less obvious, if the engrams are hosted and maintained at locations in the neural system that are close to the muscles that are guided by them, we optimize neural speed and conserve neural energy.

Speed also includes response time: We must continually respond to the current conditions of both the inner (body) and outer (surrounding) environments: As an example, while running, we have to match the mechanical speed of leg turnover with complimentary speed in our perceptions, and the speed at which we respond to those perceptions. Without this complimentary speed, we are more apt to end up injured from speed training with poor technique. It is risky to push mechanical speed faster than the speed of your KI - including proprioception and response. We can't safely run any faster than our ability to adapt the engrams to the present moment conditions.

In my experience, it is possible for us to improve the speed of neural function through *mindfulness training:* When we fully invest in this moment, we arrive with all of our "neural bandwidth". (Mental chatter distracts us and takes up bandwidth.) Mindfulness training improves our potential for proprioceptive speed and adaptive (response) speed. With maximum neural bandwidth we optimize neural function. For instance, we are better able to maintain PAGES as we conduct conventional speed-work training.

Neural Function for Speed: One Last Thing

To generate each stroke and stride, our neural system must activate specific muscle fibers in specific, well-synchronized patterns. We experience this mechanical activity as the *contraction* of muscle fibers. For instance, when your knee is bent at the top of a pedal stroke, you transmit electrical signals to contract (shorten) the muscles of your thigh (primarily your quadriceps) to extend your knee.

However, for every muscle you shorten, there is an "opposite" muscle that must *lengthen*. Lengthening a muscle requires release, relaxation. If we do not (or cannot) relax and lengthen a muscle as we are contracting its opposite, we create resistance:

- This resistance can *slow* the contractile speed of the active muscle.
- The inability to lengthen a muscle as quickly as its opposite is contracting is also a source of inefficiency - requiring that we burn more energy to overcome the resistance.
- Muscle tension that results in resistance may increase our risk of injury - to the muscles that are struggling to contract and/or to the muscles that are reluctant to lengthen.

As we pursue speed, neural function also includes our ability to quickly *relax each muscle* during the phase of the stroke/stride cycle where its contractile strength is not needed. Therefore, neural fitness - including speed - is not just focused on making muscles contract quickly, it is also focused on:

- Activating (contracting) *only* those muscles that are required for each specific phase of a stroke/stride
- Relaxing (lengthening) and *resting* all the other muscles that are not required
- Accurately synchronizing this balance between contracting and lengthening muscles

Neural Fitness: Kinetic Intelligence

To improve endurance fitness, we orchestrate the Fitness Cycle for three physiological systems:

- Metabolic
- Muscular
- Neural

We have identified the neural system as the one that responds and improves the most to training. This means that the neural system can recover and adapt to stress more readily than the metabolic or muscular. While stress to the metabolic and muscular systems often results in (hopefully minor) chemical or mechanical damage to cells, normal endurance training does not cause much (if any) actual damage to nerve cells.

When we exercise nerve cells as a means of improving fitness, we are electrically stimulating the neural system to improve its function through stronger, more enduring electrical conduction and insulation. Very significantly to us as master athletes, as we age, our neural system doesn't lose its capacity to cycle through stress, recovery and adaptation as quickly as our metabolic system does - provided we care for it and train it intelligently. Instead, our neural system may *increase* its Fitness Cycle capacity as we age.

Also, as part of the neural Adaptation Phase of the Fitness Cycle - beyond strength, endurance and speed - we are building more synaptic connections and improving the neural matrix as a whole. As we age, we continue to develop, strengthen and improve our "engram management capacity" to create, store, retrieve, activate, coordinate, synchronize, adapt and refine engrams. These are the physiological steps in developing and refining the "packets" of kinetic intelligence.

KI is unique to neural training and fitness, and it can increase significantly with age.

Our ability to craft PAGES strokes and strides certainly requires metabolic fitness and a strong neuromuscular foundation of:

- Balance (especially proprioceptive)

- Strength
- Stability
- Agility
- Mobility
- Flexibility
- Coordination

However, that ability also requires *mindfulness* so we can manage and optimize the Engram Process. As we considered earlier, neural plasticity and adaptability (again, contingent on *mindfulness*) are essential attributes we must include in our neural training to cultivate the wisdom of the aging athlete - kinetic intelligence.

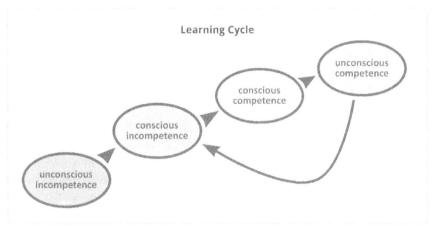

Four-Stage Learning Cycle

We cycle through four stages as we learn any new skill - from crawling on all fours as a baby, to efficient freestyle swimming, to flying a commercial airliner. As we learn each new skill, we are processing engrams. The four stages of this Learning Cycle are:

1. Unconscious Incompetence
2. Conscious Incompetence
3. Conscious Competence
4. Unconscious Competence

- In the early part of Stage 1, we are not even aware of the possibility for a potential new skill. In the later part of Stage 1, we are aware of the possibility for a new skill, but we do not know what misperceptions or incorrect actions prevent us from learning the new skill.

- In Stage 2, we identify what perceptions and actions are preventing us from acquiring that skill. (This requires humility, patience and Beginner's Mind.)

- In Stage 3, we consciously make the shifts in our perceptions and the changes in our actions that enable us to perform this new skill. This is the stage where we are step-by-step creating, storing and learning how to retrieve and activate new engrams.

- And finally, in Stage 4, we no longer have to consciously direct ourselves step-by-step through the process. The new skill is successfully embedded as engrams that we can easily retrieve, activate, coordinate and adapt. We have *embodied* this new skill.

As we learn a new skill - say, efficient freestyle swimming - we can actually be in more than one stage of the Learning Cycle simultaneously. As an example: With patience, humility and practice, we have identified the misperceptions and incorrect actions that cause our legs to sink. We have successfully created and embodied new engrams that enable us to swim and maintain fore-aft balance without excessive kicking…

…That is, *as long as we are not trying to breathe.* We are just beginning to identify and train correct head position and synchronization of breathing with the stroke. While we have been successful at developing some key elements of kinetic intelligence for efficient swimming (stroke mechanics), we are engaged in the process all over again with another key element (breathing).

This Four-Stage Learning Process is a significant part of neural training. This is a dimension to training that is unique to the neural system. Therefore our *approach* to neural training is significantly different than metabolic training. Our approach to neural training focuses on sharpening the axe of perceptive acuity - something we are already familiar with.

Neural Fitness Summary

Your neural system is a vast wiring network that transmits electrical signals in two directions:

- "Incoming" signals transmit perceptions - sense-felt experiences
- "Outgoing" signals transmit responses - actions

Conventionally, this wiring matrix is seen to connect the PNS (body) with the CNS (brain and spine)

What we identify as "intelligence" seems to be located in neurons. More specifically it is the complex *networks* of neurons that host our intelligence. A single neuron houses just one "packet" of that intelligence. In computer science terminology, we can view each neuron as housing a single "byte" of kinetic intelligence.

Our brains consist of high concentrations of neurons that are intricately connected to form vast matrixes. However our spines and even our muscles are also infused with matrixes of neurons called ganglia. An octopus has almost twice as many neurons in its arms as it does in its brain. Consequently, each arm is able to perceive, problem-solve and articulate without necessarily consulting the brain.

The presence of ganglia in our muscles suggests that much of our kinetic intelligence to generate PAGES movements is located in our bodies.

Neural fitness begins with neural function and neural plasticity. The first level of neural function is our ability to generate clear and accurate electrical signals and transmit them to the correct destination. These electrical transmissions are essential for perceiving, deciding how to respond, and actually responding.

Neural plasticity refers to our ability to learn. As endurance athletes, this is our ability to develop and refine our PAGES strokes and strides. Neural plasticity determines our capacity to build kinetic intelligence. Like neural function, neural plasticity is both perceptive and executive. We must increase our perceptive acuity before we can further improve PAGES.

If our perceptive acuity is insufficient, there is no possibility for kaizen. We will continue to respond as we have in the past. *This is why training mindfulness is always a part of neural fitness training:* We must fully occupy and engage in this present moment to maximize our perceptive acuity.

An *engram* is "A presumed encoding in neural tissue that provides a physical basis for the persistence of memory; a memory trace." Engrams are the storage files for PAGES strokes and strides, the memory files or "packets" of kinetic intelligence. They are stored in neurons - often the ganglia (groups of neurons) *embedded* in the muscle tissue, hence our experience of "muscle memory".

Neural plasticity is our ability to "process" engrams. Neural plasticity enables us to:

- create
- store
- retrieve
- activate
- coordinate
- synchronize

- and refine engrams

With each stroke and stride, we are retrieving and activating engrams, and adapting them to the conditions of the present moment. This is the essence of technique.

Neural plasticity in any specific area is contingent upon practice and training. If we don't engage our neurons in the Fitness Cycle (Stress, Recovery, Adaptation), we can't expect to gain neural fitness.

There are four elements we train for neural fitness:

- Neural strength
- Neural endurance
- Neural speed
- Kinetic intelligence

The first three - strength, endurance and speed - are familiar to anyone who has focused on conventional metabolic and muscular fitness. The fourth one - kinetic intelligence - is unique to neural fitness.

Our ability to craft PAGES strokes and strides certainly requires adequate metabolic health and fitness. It also requires a strong neuromuscular foundation of:

- Balance (especially proprioception)
- Strength
- Stability
- Agility
- Mobility
- Flexibility
- Coordination

However, that ability also requires *mindfulness* so we can manage and optimize the Engram Process. As we considered earlier, neural plasticity and adaptability (again, contingent on *mindfulness*) are essential attributes we must develop in our neural training to cultivate the wisdom of the aging athlete - kinetic intelligence

We cycle through four stages as we learn any new skill:

1. Unconscious Incompetence
2. Conscious Incompetence
3. Conscious Competence
4. Unconscious Competence

As we learn a new skill, we can actually be in multiple stages of the Learning Cycle simultaneously.

This Four-Stage Learning Process is a significant part of neural training. This is a dimension to training that is unique to the neural system. Therefore our *approach* is more essential to neural training than to metabolic training.

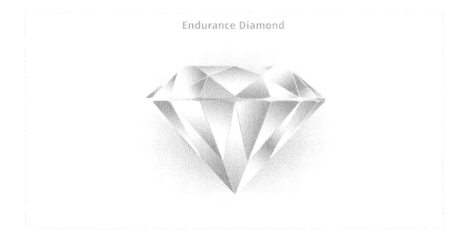

Endurance Diamond

CHAPTER SIX:
The Endurance Diamond

OK... You made it through the *tedium* of the last two chapters about neural fitness. As tedious as all of that material was, we explored the incredible multidimensional matrix that neural fitness is, including KI. There is a reward for this.

With the knowledge and insight we gained from this exploration, it's time to upgrade one of the analogies we've been using: It's time to move out of that studio with the wall of TV screens that represent the vast array of sense-felt experiences we have to monitor and respond to when we train and race at our highest potential.

In this book, with its in-depth focus on neural training, let's refine this analogy of how awareness and attention function. Let's make it more multidimensional. Instead of the wall of television monitors, let's imagine a *diamond*. In it's original rough and uncut condition, the diamond does not catch our eye. It's surface is rough and cannot play with light. It's center is dark and muddled, since the light cannot penetrate the surface. It's like a lump of coal.

A diamond begins to sparkle as the surface is cut and polished by a skilled diamond cutter. The stakes are high for the diamond cutter: S/he must inspect the diamond closely and carefully cut *facets* into the diamond's surface - paying attention to the angle and shape of each facet, and how it relates to every other facet and the overall shape of the cut diamond. The more facets the diamond has, the more the light will "dance" with it - penetrate to its center and reflect off its surfaces. It's up to the diamond cutter whether the diamond-in-the-rough becomes a jewel of light or remains just another rock.

Discovering and cutting our Endurance Diamond through zendurance training looks like this:

1. Awaken Awareness: First we awaken to a calm, still, silent, grounded and centered awareness that exists *independent* of our attention, and is *undetectable* to our attention. We awaken to this at the center of the diamond. Before we can begin to cut the facets on the rough and uncut surface of our Endurance Diamond, we must discover and awaken to this awareness deep within.
2. Locate and Occupy Awareness: When we locate and fully occupy our awareness at the center of the Endurance Diamond, we have a stable multidimensional "control center". With training, our awareness begins to "see" simultaneously in many directions. From the awareness center of our Endurance Diamond, we have the potential to direct and hold focused attention for longer duration and with higher resolution as we train and race. Proprioceptive training is a particularly effective component of neural training for awakening, and occupying awareness.
3. Create Facets of Attention: Just as the diamond cutter will carefully cut one facet at a time on the surface of the diamond, we carefully create the facets of our Endurance Diamond as we

discover and connect to more facets of our attention, especially our sense-felt experience. (Remember, sitting meditation is the exercise of maintaining awareness and attention on just the facets of sense-felt experience while breathing. We are adding many more facets to this as we train and race.)

4. Crystal Clarity: As we train and strengthen the interface of our multi-dimensional awareness with our multi-faceted attention, we learn to monitor more and more facets of our attention simultaneously. We cut and polish more and more facets in the surface of our diamond. It is no longer a diamond-in-the-rough. We are crafting a multi-faceted Endurance Diamond. The light from each carefully cut and polished facet can penetrate deep to the diamond's center. In that center, we experience the clarity of a polished, multi-faceted crystal. We gain the ability to simultaneously monitor many of those clear facets with greater accuracy.

5. Mastery as Diamond Performance: From the strength and clarity of our awareness perfectly centered in the diamond, and through the vast array of "light beams" - facets of attention - that deeply penetrate to that center, we develop the discernment to respond to those facets of our attention that most require response as each moment arises.

Brilliance arises through a highly functional Diamond.

CHAPTER SEVEN:

An Introduction to Neural Training

At First, Take it *Easy!*

Practice does not make perfect. *Perfect* practice makes perfect.

Perfect practice enables us to create and store the highest quality engrams for our PAGES strokes and strides. On the flip side, if we put in junk miles with junk technique - for instance, watching TV while pedaling away on the stationary stand - we are likely to create and store junk engrams. As master athletes, the success of our goal performances is contingent not so much on how many strokes and strides we have struggled and slogged through. It is more contingent upon the quality of the engrams we have created and stored. These engrams are the most valuable tools we will engage on race day.

To develop great PAGES technique, we have to create and store high-quality PAGES engrams. And then to reliably execute PAGES technique, we have to retrieve, activate coordinate, synchronize and adapt those engrams. (Neural function and neural strength.) To do this for hours on end, we must repeatedly retrieve and activate those engrams and constantly adapt them to the ever-changing present moment. (Neural endurance.) And we need to retrieve, activate, coordinate and synchronize those engrams quickly and adapt them instantly to the present moment conditions. (Neural speed.)

In the beginning, to create those high-quality engrams we focus on the biomechanics of each stroke and stride. We are able to do this most effectively (especially when we are new to neural training) when we train with curiosity and patience, *at low metabolic intensity*. Here's why:

Our metabolic system functions to provide the active nerves and muscles with an *ideal operating environment*. As intensity increases, the metabolic system is no longer able to maintain ideal conditions for that operating environment. It becomes *hostile* due to chemical changes. Imagine that you are running on a treadmill in a room. At low metabolic intensity, conditions in the room are ideal: A cool temperature, plenty of oxygen and pH balanced (that is, not too acidic or alkaline). At high metabolic intensity, the room get much hotter, there is less oxygen and you feel the burn of acid.

The challenges and demands (stresses) imposed on the neural system to learn and execute optimum biomechanics should not initially be combined with a hostile operating environment - such as the chemical stress of high metabolic demand, or the mechanical stress of high muscular demand. And remember, that those challenges and demands pertain to all three neural functions: perceptive, responsive and executive.

In the early stages, combining neural intensity (to develop efficiency) with metabolic intensity (to develop speed) will usually retard technique development. It takes a lot of faith and patience on the part of the ambitious athlete to forego the compromised operating environment of high metabolic intensity while creating and storing quality engrams of PAGES technique.

With respect to the Four-Stage Learning Cycle: First, you must awaken to what is *not* working, to what can be improved. This is the progression from Stage 1 (Unconscious Incompetence) to Stage 2 (Conscious Incompetence). It requires a lot of patience, curiosity *and humility* to take this step. You must be willing to discover. That is easier when you are not hell-bent on high-level performance.

Next, you must make a *conscious effort* to change the pattern - that is, to create and store high-quality engrams: Perfect practice! (Stage 2 to 3 - Conscious Competence.) Finally - with patience, perseverance and consistency, you no longer need to make a conscious effort to execute the optimal stroke or stride. (Stage 3 to 4 - Unconscious Competence.) Now you have successfully created and stored the high-quality engram and you can retrieve and activate it with ease. Now you can start to ramp up the metabolic intensity.

Remember, at high metabolic intensity and - to a slightly lesser extent - high muscular intensity, every progression in this 4-step learning process is far more difficult. Imagine you are trying to learn something new in a classroom that is too hot or too cold, and too dark - an environment that is not conducive to learning.

During this progression - especially from Conscious Competence (Stage 3) to Unconscious Competence (Step 4) - you are orchestrating a biological adaptation called *"myelination"*. Again, this adaptation occurs best in a supportive metabolic environment.

Myelination

Perfect practice involves repeating an efficient movement pattern repeatedly and correctly to create, store and refine those "packets" of kinetic intelligence - engrams. This neural exercise stimulates the adaptive process *"myelination"*. Myelination is the biological process by which myelin is formed around nerve cells (neurons) to form the insulative *sheath*.

Myelin sheathing functions much the same as insulation on an electrical wire. Specifically, it forms around the long shaft, or axon, of the neuron. This insulation enables the nerve cell to transmit information (as electrical pulses) better, and allows for more complex neural network processes - like the efficient movement patterns of kinetic intelligence.

This adaptive process of myelination takes about *two weeks* - given consistent, patient, mindful practice. Keep in mind that this two weeks is for *one specific neural pathway*. As kaizen athletes, we are constantly learning and refining. Hence the process of myelination is also ongoing: We may be completing myelination (*and* the 4-Stage Learning Cycle) for one specific engram, while just awakening to and introducing another engram.

Progressing through the Four-Stage Learning Cycle is a rigorous activity. We often associate rigorous activity with *work*. However, learning and work are not always compatible.

The Power of Play

A musician does not *"work"* the violin, or *"work"* a symphony. Instead, she *plays* the violin, *plays* the symphony. So... what's the difference?

In the context of *work*, we are engaged in an activity whose purpose is to bring about a specific result. From the beginning, we are focused on the outcome.

In the context of *play*, we are engaged in an activity that is free from such expectations. Without the pressure to secure a specific result, we are free to wander, to experiment and explore, to be creative and intuitive. We are empowered to *learn*.

If the point of a symphony was the end result - the final chord - then the most heralded conductors would be the ones who drove the orchestra fastest through each composition. Instead we appreciate the conductor who empowers the orchestra to *play* the symphony in a way that touches us deeply, that helps both the musicians and the audience to rediscover the infinite potential of our experience-ability.

I have guided thousands of people through the process of learning to swim. A foundation in my approach with each client is to facilitate the activity of *play*. The focus is not to "*get across the goddamn pool*". The focus is to awaken to the myriad sense-felt experiences of how we move through the water:

- Where and when do we feel smooth hydrodynamics?
- Where and when do we feel the disturbance of drag?
- When do we feel that we are struggling?
- When do we feel that we are PAGES?

"*I am not your swim coach. The* water *is your swim coach.*"

We learn most effectively when we are free from the pressures and expectations of results. (That is work.) We learn most effectively when we engage and interface completely with what is arising in this moment with *all of our resources* - our myriad sense-felt experiences, our astute intellectual observations, our deep and powerful feelings, as well as our *curiosity, creativity and intuition*. We do this without attachment to a specific result. (That is play.)

In Book One, we explored Approach as the process of sharpening the axe of perceptive acuity. We identified Beginner's Mind as a mindfulness skill that enhances that Approach. We associate both play and Beginner's Mind with children. In our life cycle, we learn fastest in childhood. If we *allow* ourselves to play as adults, we can continue to learn quickly.

When you train, it is fine to have goals or intended results to guide each session. However, when you *trust the playful learning process* without fixating on those goals, you are more apt to maximize return on your aerobic investment.

Mindful play is a key to neural training. It is the most effective way to refine our Endurance Diamond.

The Golden Opportunity: Recovery Sessions

The optimal environment to begin neural training is during easy-paced *recovery sessions*. We are not fixated on producing some metabolically measurable outcome that will distract us from:

- Investing and seamlessly interfacing our awareness with many facets of high-resolution attention. (Developing and improving our Endurance Diamond)

- Engaging this interface to create and store high-quality engrams.

- Training our skill to recall, activate and refine these engrams, and to coordinate and synchronize them with each other. (For example a leg stride with an arm swing.)

Recovery sessions provide the perfect "playground" for the patient investigative process of challenging perceptive acuity without the expectation of immediate answers, or the drive to meet metrics. We create a safe place to *play* - to relax, be curious, and to discover. In this no-pressure context, and in an ideal metabolic operating environment, we are able to challenge and improve our perceptions by fully interfacing our awareness with many facets of high-resolution attention. Hence, we are more apt to *awaken* to the opportunities for pursuing mastery - moving from Stage 1 to Stage 2 - from unconscious to conscious.

To maximize return on your training investment, approach recovery sessions with a curiosity-based focus - even an *artistic* commitment to - perfect technique. This is your *opportunity for discovery*. It is your opportunity to further facet and polish your Endurance Diamond. Discovery requires the humility, patience and curiosity of Beginner's Mind to *awaken* to what we don't know - to move from Stage 1 to Stage 2 in the Four-Stage Learning Cycle.

This is such radical shift from our usual approach of "hitting the numbers", and our disdain for weakness (incompetence). To get the most out of recovery sessions, we uncover and embrace our weaknesses as opportunities for discovery, rather than denying them or attacking them with exertion.

As we strengthen this approach during our recovery sessions, we become more familiar with how to cut and polish the facets of our Endurance Diamond: We are gradually more able to occupy and engage a highly vigilant awareness at the center of the Diamond. This enables us to create and to monitor more facets of attention to efficiency. With this more functional Endurance Diamond, we will maintain PAGES during our "more important" higher-intensity training and racing.

It takes considerable neural fitness and mindfulness skill to develop such a high-performance Endurance Diamond. And it happens best in an ideal metabolically produced operating environment.

Introducing Intensity

As we improve our Endurance Diamond and gain proficiency (starting with *patience*) with the 4-Stage Practice Progression, it is OK to fold in the challenge of performing efficient technique in the less-than-ideal operating environment of higher metabolic intensity. (That is, if going faster is aligned with your goals.)

During high intensity intervals, it is imperative that we *constantly monitor the quality of our PAGES technique*. We do this:

- For the sake of efficiency
- To guard from injury
- For our commitment to kaizen

If maintaining and improving PAGES technique is the top priority, high intensity interval sets must be governed by our capacity to maintain PAGES.

Certainly we can target a specific level of metabolic intensity during our intervals, tempo training, and long sessions. However, if the technique erodes, we must restructure the training session to enable PAGES first. This requires discernment to know when the technique erodes, as well as the reserve and patience to *stay within the neural limits* - even if we have not reached the targeted metabolic intensity.

The initial introduction of high intensity is best implemented through very brief intervals with generous recovery between each. (This type of interval training is called Neuromuscular Intervals.) Again, *the primary focus must be perfect technique!*

Metrics: Monitoring and Evaluating Technique

The most common metrics for structuring metabolic Energy System Training (EST) are:

- Distance
- Time
- Metabolic Intensity (Level of metabolic activity typically correlated to blood lactate level)
- Velocity (Correlated to metabolic intensity)
- Power output (Correlated to metabolic intensity)

After blood lactate testing, velocity, power output, and heart rate can be correlated to determine intensity. The focus in EST is to maintain a specific metabolic rate of intensity for a given duration (as either time or distance). These metrics *govern* the training - meaning that the athlete must focus on maintaining the prescribed level of metabolic intensity for the given duration.

Likewise, technique-focused Neuro-Muscular Training (NMT) can also includes metrics. These metrics are:

- Stroke/stride length (SL)
- Cadence (number of stroke/strides per unit of time or amount of time per stroke/stride)
- Rate of Perceived Exertion (RPE)
- Duration (Time and/or Distance)

The two parameters unique to NMT are stroke/stride length (SL) and cadence. SL is an incremental way of measuring *distance*. Likewise, cadence is an incremental way of measuring *time*. Therefore, if you know your SL, your cadence, and the total number of strokes/strides (frequency), you can calculate the total time (duration) and distance.

This incremental method of monitoring distance and time enables the athlete (and coach) to closely monitor and evaluate the quality and efficiency of technique through a sequence of "now moments". Additionally, this incremental measure can be compared to (*but is not governed by*) metabolic intensity. This comparison enables athlete and coach to evaluate PAGES while striving for one of these goals:

- Lowering metabolic intensity at a specific stroke/stride length and cadence and distance
- Maintaining metabolic intensity at an increased SL and/or cadence and/or distance

Achieving either one of these goals indicates a higher level of efficiency, or the ability to sustain a specific level of efficiency over a longer duration.

Establishing a "Baseline Experience" of PAGES Technique

Immediately before an athlete commences a challenging endurance session, a tempo session or - most importantly - a high-intensity interval session, it is imperative to establish a *current baseline experience* of PAGES technique and *to prepare the neuromuscular system to maintain that technique*. Remember, high-intensity training is "high-stakes": There is an elevated risk of injury - especially while running. Playing successfully at this level requires KI and PAGES technique that reduces the risk of injury.

This baseline experience enables the athlete to then constantly monitor and evaluate technique efficiency - ideally during *each stroke or stride* - always comparing to an "embodied standard". This "embodied standard" is encoded in our neurons as the current set of engrams. These engrams function as the governor, the standard for setting the training session parameters: If the technique erodes from this standard, we must modify the metrics through some combination of these changes:

- Reduce cadence/tempo
- Reduce stroke/stride length
- Reduce duration of interval
- Increase recovery duration
- Decrease recovery intensity (rest easier)

The purpose for modifying these metrics is to regain our capacity to retrieve and activate the engrams for our optimum PAGES stroke/stride - *and to regain our capacity to adapt these engrams to the higher metabolic level of challenge*. How do we know when we have regained these capacities? By our *feeling*. That is, we know because we *feel* that we have returned to PAGES. We can also monitor the NMT metrics listed above.

Remember, this neuromuscular preparation for establishing a baseline of PAGES technique *significantly reduces the risk of injury*. For this gain alone, it is worth the investment of time, awareness and attention.

Proceed Patiently

Mentally, we must first *patiently orchestrate the Approach*:

- "Sharpen the Axe of Awareness"
- Activate Beginner's Mind
- Activate Finalist's Mind
- Stimulate curiosity, and yes, creativity
- Be Here Now!
- Occupy and engage the Endurance Diamond - our ability to monitor and respond to the myriad facets of attention for PAGES technique

Collectively, these steps enable us to summon and engage full awareness and attention. In a single word: *mindfulness*.

This preparation might also include:

- A contemplation of the session structure and purpose
- Identifying a sequence of sensation-based technique focal points for the session
- Identifying the return on investment that this session can yield for upcoming goals
- A reflection on all that you are grateful for, all the assets and skills that have delivered you to this opportunity

Get Started

We can begin the actual physical activity with a patient, mindful warm-up that also serves as a *body-mind tune-in*.

I begin every session at a *very* relaxed and gentle pace, (dare I say "*lazy*"?) as I fully engage my proprioceptivity and sensation-based body awareness to bring my Endurance Diamond online. This awareness-attention interface includes being present with any feelings of stiffness, soreness, etc. My RPE during this initial activation begins at 1-2 and gently increases to 4-5 (on a scale of 1-10) - usually over the course of 10-20 minutes. (At age 60, a patient and gradual warm-up is mandatory for me.) As I do most of my quality training in the morning, it can take longer (20 minutes) to adequately warm-up, compared to training later in the day (10 minutes).

I am aware of each and every breath - initially keeping my breath slow and deep. Beginning with breath awareness establishes a context of mindfulness training right from the start. *Every single endurance training session* can serve as an effective mindfulness training session. Interfacing mindfulness training with endurance training will never compromise the potential for athletic improvement. It can only enhance it.

I also focus on pelvic core engagement and stability during every session. This is key to efficient biomechanics in every endurance sport. (Pelvic core engagement is also the source for circulating chi energy.)

As my metabolic rate gradually elevates, the synovial fluid begins to lubricate my joints and the increased blood flow and body temperature optimize the metabolic "operating environment" for my muscles and connective tissues. These *gradual* metabolic changes are usually sufficient to dissolve the feelings of stiffness and soreness, as I optimize the operating environment. Simply "pushing through" these feelings with impatient force can lead to injury.

During this neuromuscular and metabolic warm-up, I focus on elements of PAGES through sensation-based focal points for that specific sport, which always include pelvic core engagement and stability. Next, if I am going to perform intervals at or above lactate threshold, I perform some drills to emphasize specific elements of PAGES biomechanics. Between each drill repetition, I perform some easy-to-moderate "whole-stroke/stride" swim/bike/running to integrate the awareness gained in the drill, using focal points.

So, let's consider…

Drills

"Drill: A tool used to bore holes, usually accomplished by a rotating, cutting bit."

Intriguing that we use this same word to identify short exercises - specific repetitive cycles of movement - to improve technique. The similarity? In endurance sports, we use drills to challenge perceptive capacity and mindfulness - to *pierce* through the veil of unconsciousness. The drill serves *as a tool* to investigate some element of our PAGES. It helps us get to the absolute center of our Endurance Diamond.

In the context of endurance sports, drills present us with a challenge, a problem: To solve this problem, we will draw upon and challenge some element of a PAGES movement. A drill is challenging because we voluntarily place some limit or constraint upon ourselves to create the problem.

The purpose of *playing the drill game* is not to "get it right" and move on. And, there are *no metabolic metrics* governing the execution of a drill - no "hitting the numbers". Rather, a drill is a puzzle. It involves some degree of trial and error, of *not-knowing*. It requires patience and curiosity - even *creativity*. Solving the puzzle involves the creative process of *questioning*. A drill serves to *challenge perceptive capacity*. It encourages us to *be creative in the questing and investigation* as we seek a solution.

To increase the power and function of our Endurance Diamond, we are constantly cutting and polishing new facets. Drills serve as great tools for that cutting and polishing.

Again, a drill often places some kind of *constraint* on the normal repetitive activity. It poses some kind of challenge. (Constraints are always an invitation to be creative.) As an example, let's consider "Fist Drill" in swimming: Swimming with your palm closed is a constraint, a challenge. Specifically, here are two challenges offered by "Fist Drill":

- Can you still effectively "grip" the water with a well-positioned forearm (often identified as Early Vertical Forearm), rather than relying solely on the much smaller surface area of your palm?

- Can you still breathe easily without pushing down with the palm of your hand to lift your head at the moment of breath?

With any drill, it is essential to specifically identify the puzzle we are seeking to solve. This directs us to interface our awareness with specific facets of attention - to *challenge our perceptive capacity* and enhance the performance of the Endurance Diamond. Playing with drills is not about conquest, not about "mind over matter", where the mind will somehow force the body to "*do it right*".

This puzzling process requires *teamwork* between mind and body to create and store high-quality engrams - the interface of awareness with specific facets of attention. Our bodies are very intelligent - if and when we can suspend our fixation on results. Our minds are vital for observation and awareness. However, fixating on a desired outcome occupies bandwidth in our awareness and diminishes the performance of our Endurance Diamond.

As a musician hones the craft of *playing* her instrument, she invests time, energy, curiosity and creativity in practicing scales and drills. She does not practice a specific scale or drill one time and then move on. The patient musician returns again and again to the "puzzle".

There is no rush to get somewhere. Slowly, over weeks, months and years, she hones the *craft* of her unique musicianship through the engram process. In the context of athletics, we often overlook the *craft* of our sport and the engram process. We focus only on achieving the goals.

When you are drilling, stay curious, and be patient. Play. Be creative. Focus on making your Endurance Diamond more brilliant. While the ultimate objective is to create and refine engrams that improve some element of your PAGES, you can only achieve this by interfacing your awareness with many facets of your attention to improve your perceptive capacity - especially your *proprioceptive* capacity. In this complete interface, there is no dominance of mind or body, because there is no difference or distinction between them.

All of us have some aversion and impatience to drills in our training. Why? Because drill work doesn't immediately affect distance, speed, power output, etc. We aren't accumulating volume or intensity in the way we do when we are executing intervals or sustained, long duration efforts. "*When will I measure with hard numbers what I have accomplished?*"

Patience, patience. Drills - when used effectively as *tools* - accelerate the 4-Stage Progression of learning technique. Drill-play (a better context than drill-work) is a key component of effective training - maximizing the return for our investment of awareness, attention, time and energy.

Returning to our diamond analogy: Your awareness is seated in the center of the diamond. You can imagine that practicing drills is like carefully cutting and polishing new facets in the rough surface.

Finishing Touches on the *Living* Baseline Experience of PAGES Technique

Finally, to complete my Baseline Experience, I may perform 3-6 brief sprints (20-30 seconds each) with my very best technique: posture, alignment, precision, biomechanics, grace, ease, efficiency, seamlessness, relaxation. I allow for plenty of recovery between each sprint. This final phase of preparation maximizes neuromuscular recruitment, so that I am engaging more muscle fibers for each PAGES stroke/stride.

I have now established a vivid and *living* Baseline Experience of PAGES technique - a *standard, a benchmark*. It is freshly imprinted in my neuromuscular *kinetic intelligence:* I have located, retrieved and activated the necessary engrams from storage. As I progress through my *neural* training session, I will compare each stoke/stride to this baseline and strive to attain (or surpass) my standard with each. Naturally, I allow for slight deviations from this standard. These are a consequence of pushing the limits - creating adequate stress to stimulate adaptation. The *art* is knowing how much deviation to allow for. (Hint: *Be conservative!*)

The vigilance to successfully monitor and evaluate PAGES technique during challenging training sessions - especially high-intensity interval training - arises from mindfulness. Mindfulness is essential for effective Neuro-Muscular Training.

Perfect Technique?

Is there an ultimate perfect technique? Is there a perfect stride or stroke that can be bottled up, branded and sold? A perfect package of engrams that we can extract, patent, duplicate and then inject? Is there a *Holy Grail* for the running stride, the pedaling stroke, the swim stroke?

No. ...And yes.

No, there is no one single stride or stroke biomechanic that is universally perfect for everybody. Even if we had the technology to do so, there is no perfect set of engrams that we could encode into each athlete to instantly transform all of us so that we could swim like Michael Phelps *and* bike like Peter Sagan *and* run like Meb Keflezighi. The reasons for this are simple. Everybody is different:

- different proportions, height, weight
- different degrees of stability, agility, mobility, flexibility
- different aerobic capacities - and therefore sustainable paces
- different goals and distances

Even for *one body*, there is no fixed and permanent perfect stride or stroke. We are constantly refining the engrams. And, in *each moment*, we must adapt our current "master engrams" for each single stride or stroke. We are striving to express the *perfect stride* for this present moment - over and over again. Even in the most uniform and consistent environment, we are still adapting each stroke/stride to slight changes - both internal and external.

For instance, in running, you adapt your running engrams to external factors to optimize your alliance with gravity and maximize your efficiency:

- topography
- terrain/surface
- pace
- distance
- metabolic intensity
- altitude
- temperature
- wind…

All of these external factors (along with the many internal factors) will affect your most efficient running stride - *in each moment*. *Each* stride, *each* stroke is unique. Each optimal stroke/stride must be crafted to interface with the present moment. Integration implies harmony, not the dominance of "mind over matter".

Technique is "Mind IN Matter".

The one single unchanging, eternally enduring constant? Gravity. Gravity is the greatest guide in our quest for the perfect stride and stroke. When we bring mindfulness and neural fitness to our alliance with gravity through proprioception, we can maximize the return on our aerobic investment.

CHAPTER EIGHT:

Conclusion

Introduction

Endurance, strength and speed are the conventional pursuits of endurance fitness. In other words, through the Fitness Cycle, we seek to improve athletic performance by targeting adaptation in these capacities. However, as master athletes, it is *kinetic intelligence* that yields the most promising discoveries, improvements *and adaptations* we can benefit from on the kaizen path. In the Fitness Cycle, KI improves through adaptation *by training the neural system*. It is not an adaptive response of the metabolic or muscular systems.

In this book, we have explored neural fitness and its relevance and benefit to overall endurance fitness and athletic performance. We have investigated kinetic intelligence as the arena of infinite potential for improvement, even as we experience a decline in aerobic capacity. Again, KI is unique to the neural system.

It's All About Bandwidth

Our capacity to build kinetic intelligence is contingent upon neural plasticity, or adaptability. This adaptability determines how readily we can learn: With neural plasticity, we are able to accelerate the Engram Process to optimize PAGES for our strokes and strides. (Wow!! It may not require ten thousand repetitions after all!) This is true not only for building great swim, bike or run technique, but for *every skill and technique in our lives*. This includes occupational and relational skills.

Neural plasticity - in every area of our lives - requires both perceptive and executive acuity.

To improve anything in our lives, we have to *start where we are Here and* Now. Without *perceptive* acuity, we cannot clearly observe, assess or respond to what is occurring in this moment. We need that perceptive acuity both internally (in our own bodies), and externally (the surrounding environment). We rely on both inner and outer perceptions that are clear and accurate to create and refine PAGES engrams, and to adapt those engrams to the current conditions.

As athletes, a significant element of our internal perception is proprioception. Proprioception requires a tremendous amount of *bandwidth* in the neural system. If we are consuming significant neural bandwidth with judgments, desires, fears, distractions, etc., we are diminishing our potential for neural plasticity.

Without *executive* acuity, we cannot express the engrams with precision, alignment, grace, efficiency and seamlessness. Proprioception is again paramount to this executive process, as well as the perceptive process. We must devote adequate neural bandwidth to this incredibly complex task.

Another essential asset for the kaizen path of mastery is the Diamond. As master athletes, we have focused specifically on the Endurance Diamond. However, we can create, engage and refine this Diamond of Mastery in any and every area of our lives. To do so, we must first awaken and anchor our awareness at the center of the Diamond. Next, we must interface our awareness with the myriad facets of attention that comprise our experience in this moment.

A highly functional Diamond requires a deep and rich interface of awareness and attention. Specifically, we must interface our awareness with the facets of our sense-felt experience as it is unfolding in this moment. Along with those sense-felt facets, we can also interface with *relevant* thoughts and feelings.

Our capacity to steadfastly occupy a vigilant awareness and to deeply interface that awareness with such a vast and complex array of *selected and relevant* facets of attention requires tremendous neural bandwidth.

What is the most essential skill for generating and maintaining adequate neural bandwidth? Mindfulness.

And what is mindfulness? It is the ability that arises from our vigilant and grounded awareness to invest and direct our *"attention in a particular way, on purpose, in the moment non-judgmentally"*. (From Jon Kabat-Zinn's definition of mindfulness, included in Chapter 1.)

Mindfulness is our skill and our strength to BE HERE NOW in this moment, exactly as it is. Mindfulness includes the indispensable skill of *neural housekeeping:* Maintaining adequate neural bandwidth to brilliantly engage the Diamond of Mastery.

Foundation of Neural Training: Mindfulness Training

Neural fitness training begins with *training mindfulness skills* that enable us to arrive in each moment of our training sessions with adequate neural bandwidth. This is essential for us to maximize return on our aerobic investment. And it is essential for us to live healthy and functional kaizen lives. Therefore…

Before we move on to the specifics of training neural endurance, strength and speed for athletic performance, we will pause, once again, to *sharpen the axe*. We will do this by investigating and developing specific mindfulness skills to increase our neural bandwidth, function and plasticity.

In Book 3, *"Training Mindfulness Skills"*, we explore nine *"Attitudes of Mindfulness"* that Jon Kabat-Zinn has identified. We consider how each is relevant to kaizen-durance. We explore how to engage and exercise each of these attitudes/skills through our daily zendurance training sessions, our goal races, and - most importantly - in our daily lives outside of sports.

And then, in Book 4 *"A Guide to Neural Training"*, we will return to the specifics of neural training as master endurance athletes.

ABOUT THE AUTHOR

Shane Eversfield is Founder and C.E.W.* of Kaizen-durance. A degree in Modern Dance, 40 years of T'ai Chi practice and a lifelong passion for mindful movement and "kinetic intelligence" fuel his innovative fusion study of applied kinesiology and mindfulness. As an athlete, author, educator, artist and coach, he has earned the respect of many endurance athletes and coaches the world over.

Eversfield teaches over 200 classes and clinics every year in swimming, cycling, running and Kaizen Skills. He has trained and educated coaches and athletes in the US, Europe and Asia. He is based out of Island Health and Fitness in Ithaca, NY, and is a staff coach for the Total Immersion Swim Studio in New Paltz, NY.

Now 60+ years young, he continues his personal Kaizen path and the cultivation of kinetic intelligence through his daily endurance arts practice. He enjoys multi-day triathlons and ultra running events each year. and continues to quietly slip past his perceived limits. Shane regards himself as a modern-day "traditional" martial artist – deeply committed to the craft of mindful movement – rather than an as athlete.

Visit https://kaizen-durance.com/ for information about:

– Kaizen-durance® Endurance Arts Camps, Clinics, Classes: Locally (Ithaca, NY) and internationally
– Kaizen Skills: Fitness for Your Life Programs
– Bio for Shane Eversfield, Founder and C.E.W.* of Kaizen-durance

* C.E.W.: Chief Endurance Whisperer